Play Ball Like the Pros

Discard

Discard

Play Ball Like the Pros

TIPS FOR KIDS FROM 20 BIG LEAGUE STARS

STEVEN KRASNER

Ω
PEACHTREE
ATLANTA

Ω

Published by
PEACHTREE PUBLISHERS
1700 Chattahoochee Avenue
Atlanta, Georgia 30318-2112
www.peachtree-online.com

Text © 2002, 2010 Steven Krasner

Cover design by Maureen Withee
Interior design by Melanie McMahon Ives

Manufactured in the United States of America

10 9 8 7 6 5 4 3 2 1
Second Edition

Library of Congress Cataloging-in-Publication Data

Krasner, Steven.
    Play ball like the pros : tips for kids from 20 big league stars / written by Steven Krasner.
        p. cm.
    Summary: "Nearly two dozen professional baseball players provide insights into how they
prepare for and play the game"--Provided by publisher.
    ISBN 978-1-56145-535-5 / 1-56145-535-0
    1. Baseball for children--Juvenile literature. I. Title.
    GV880.4.K72 2009
    796.357'2--dc22
                                    2009034080

For my father, Julius, who passed down to me
his passion for the game of baseball—
and for my son, Jeffrey, a better player than both of us,
who has carried on the family tradition

—S. K.

CONTENTS

★★★★★★★★★★★★★★★★★★★★★★★★★★★★★★★★

BATTER UP!

Game 4 ...

**The 2008 World Series, Tampa Bay Rays versus the
Philadelphia Phillies ...**

The Phillies' Ryan Howard swings and connects squarely, sending the baseball soaring up, up and away, over the fence at Citizens Bank Park in Philadelphia. It's a home run!

Obviously, that had to be a very special moment for Howard, playing in his first World Series. A few innings later, Howard added another home run, his two blasts in the same game giving the Phillies a resounding victory, ultimately helping Philadelphia claim its first World Series crown since 1980.

But in a way, Howard had lived these moments many times before back on the playing fields in his home town of St. Louis, MO, when he would pretend that he had just clouted a World Series home run.

His dream became a reality.

Probably every player who wears a big league uniform shares that same childhood dream. And it's a pretty sure bet that the big leaguers of the future are running around bases in a field somewhere right now, dreaming similar dreams.

Of course, it takes more than just dreams to become a good baseball player. In this book, you'll find great tips from twenty big league stars to help you improve your skills. The players will also share their own childhood memories of playing ball, as well as the lessons they began learning at a very young age.

You may be surprised to find out that becoming a successful ballplayer isn't just about skills, or being born with superstar talent. It also has a lot to do with using your brain. Being smart on the baseball field—which includes the ability to make quick, accurate decisions—can help your team win. In each chapter of this book, there will be a tricky situation to test your baseball brain, as well as the best possible solution.

Sometimes, of course, things don't go well for even the smartest players. This can lead to some unusual—and occasionally embarrassing—moments that you'll also find recounted in this book. Baseballs have been known to bounce off an outfielder's head. Or roll into a beverage cup on the field. Or take bad hops at the very worst times.

But as they say around the big league diamonds, "That's baseball." It's a great game. At any age.

Play ball!

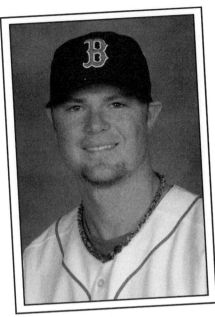

STRETCHING AND WARMING UP

JON LESTER

When a game begins, all eyes are on the pitcher. He starts his **windup**, his arm whips around, and he throws the ball to the plate. Even though that's the first pitch of the game, the act of throwing the ball didn't start just then for the pitcher. His preparation began much earlier that day.

In this chapter, Jon Lester explains how to warm up properly before each game. He describes how and why a pitcher stretches and how he gets his arm loose even before he plays catch.

What do you do when you first get onto the field?

You don't want to start stretching without moving around first. I like to jog a little bit and to do some "moving stretching," especially if it's cold outside, because I want to get the blood flowing a little bit. And then I get into my routine—some basic stretching of my arms, shoulders, and back.

What types of "moving stretching" do you do?

You walk and stretch. You take a couple of steps and do a stretch for your quadriceps [muscle on the front of the thigh]. You grab a foot, pull it up behind you and stretch your quad, and then you put it down, take a couple of more steps, and you do a quad stretch with the other leg. You do a lunge, and then you rotate your upper body so you can loosen up your back. Stuff like that.

What kind of stretches do you do for your arms?

You pull your arm across your chest, holding the elbow to pull it across. You can do arm circles, holding your arms out and rotating them in circles. You can stretch your forearms by holding your arm out with your elbow straight and your palm turned up, then pulling down on your wrist and fingers with the other hand.

If you throw with your arm, why is it necessary to stretch your legs, too?

Well, you don't throw with just your arm, you throw with your whole body. Your body is a lot of parts working as one unit to throw the ball, so you have to make sure that your whole body is loose, and not just your arm. Otherwise, you can get hurt. If you don't loosen up all over, you can pull a muscle in your legs or your back or somewhere else. Always make sure your whole body is loose before you get going so you don't injure yourself.

Once you have stretched, do you just then get on the mound and throw as hard as you can?

I don't get on the mound right after stretching.

I stretch, then I do a **long-toss** throwing program until I feel that I'm loose enough to get on the mound. I start playing catch at a distance of 60 feet and then move back to 120 and sometimes as far as 200 feet. It just depends on how I'm feeling that day and how well I'm loosening up. If I'm getting loose pretty quickly, then I play catch for a fairly short period of time. I don't want to wear out my arm playing long toss. I want to save it for the game.

When it's colder out, I'll play long toss for a longer period of time to make sure I'm loose before I start warming up in the bullpen.

When you do get on the mound, do you throw at 100 percent of your speed right from the first warm-up toss?

It depends. For me, every start is different.

Sometimes you start warming up and you feel like you're throwing backwards, and you can't get loose; you can't find a rhythm, and the ball's not coming out of your hand very well. And then there are other starts where as soon as you lift your leg up to throw a pitch in the bullpen you're throwing at 100 miles an hour.

So it just depends on how your body feels, how your arm feels, and how quickly you're able to get loose. These things dictate how your bullpen session goes.

When you make your first few pitches, do you just try to throw the ball down the middle or do you try to hit the corners right away?

I have my normal routine that I've developed over the years. In my warm-up, I throw to the sides of the plate. I warm up with fastballs first and then go to **off-speed** stuff, so I'm able to develop a little bit of a rhythm before I start trying to spin **breaking balls** and throw **changeups**.

All of this preparation helps me get loose and get my body ready to pitch.

For kids eight to twelve, is there a best type of grip for throwing the ball?

Just throw it. I didn't know anything about pitching when I was that age. Don't worry about **four-seam** or **two-seam** grips. Just learn how to throw a ball.

I mean, it's hard enough just to throw a baseball straight. So when you're eight to twelve years old, you should just be having fun when you play. I don't really care how you grip the ball. Just grab it and throw it. Whatever feels comfortable. If you like throwing it with a two-seam grip, then throw it that way. If you like throwing it with a four-seam grip, throw it like that. At that age it doesn't matter, as long as you're throwing a baseball and having fun doing it.

How steady should your head be when you pitch a baseball?

I don't think it's important. Look at [former Red Sox teammate Hideki] Okajima. He doesn't look at home plate until after he throws the ball.

It's the same answer I gave about whether you should throw a four-seam or a two-seam fastball. Do whatever feels comfortable for you, whatever works for you. If you feel comfortable looking at the ground and then throwing the ball, that's fine.

I don't like the whole "fitting into a mold" thing. There's no mold. Everybody has their own throwing motion. When you try to make a guy throw like someone else—fit into a mold—that's when athletes get hurt. Every kid has to have his niche and find what works for him. That's what makes us individuals and makes us special. You can't just mold a kid after somebody and say, "Go get 'em." That might not be something that works for him.

At what point do you know everything you need to know about yourself and the game?

The more you play and the longer you play, the more you learn. You've got guys like John Smoltz who have been in the big leagues for more than twenty years. He's over forty and has played baseball for all his adult life, and he's still learning. Every day is a learning curve. Every day you can learn something new about yourself and the opponent and what you're able to do on a baseball field. The good players are able to do that. The mediocre players are the ones who are stubborn and don't learn and go out there and just "do their thing."

    GLOSSARY

Breaking ball: A pitch with a lot of spin. The most common type of breaking ball is a curveball.

Changeup: A pitch that is meant to look like a fastball when it leaves the pitcher's hand but in fact arrives at the plate at a slower speed.

Four-seam grip: A grip of the baseball in which the fingers are positioned across, not with, the four seams of the ball. This grip produces a rotation that keeps the ball moving in a straight line.

Long toss: Playing catch at a long distance.

Off-speed: Slower than a fastball.

Two-seam grip: A grip of the baseball in which the fingers are placed along the seams of the ball, causing it to tail when thrown. A two-seam pitch thrown by a right-handed pitcher will tail in toward a right-handed hitter.

Windup: The pitcher's motion when there are no runners on base. One or both feet are on the rubber and he faces the hitter head-on as he begins his delivery.

Extremely Well Armed!

Most pitchers have to make sure just one of their arms is especially stretched and loose for an appearance in a game.

But not Greg Harris.

Harris made big league history, pitching as both a right-hander and a left-hander in the same inning of a game at Montreal's Olympic Stadium on September 28, 1995. It was something that Harris had always wanted to do. He was ambidextrous, which means he was able to perform certain tasks, such as using a fork, equally well with each hand.

As a member of the Boston Red Sox, Harris pitched right-handed. But during batting practice, he would catch balls and throw them in from the outfield using his left arm. He had a rare six-finger glove that allowed him to use it on either hand. When Harris was traded to the Montreal Expos in 1995, his manager, Felipe Alou, decided it was time for an ambidextrous pitcher to appear in the big leagues.

The Cincinnati Reds were ahead of the Expos by six runs when Harris was called in to pitch the ninth inning. As a right-hander, he retired Reggie Sanders, a right-handed hitter, on a routine ground ball to shortstop.

Then the Reds had a couple of left-handed hitters come to the plate. Harris shifted positions and stood on the pitching rubber as a left-hander. His first left-handed pitch was wild and it sailed to the backstop. The next three weren't much better and he walked Hal Morris on four straight pitches.

But then Harris settled down. He retired the next batter, Ed Taubensee, on a tapper in front of the plate. Then, as a right-handed pitcher, he set down Bret Boone on a bouncer back to the mound. The big leagues' first ambidextrous pitcher didn't give up a single run!

★★★★★★★★★★★★★★★★★★★★★★★★★★

HERE'S THE SITUATION

The sun is out, it's very hot, and you've been running around all day with your friends. Maybe you've even gone swimming.

You're tired, and you're pitching in a game that night.

You don't want to stretch.

Does the heat make you loose enough that you don't need to stretch before the game? Should you not warm up, figuring that the fewer pitches you throw, the longer you'll be able to pitch in the game?

HERE'S THE SOLUTION

Always stretch! No matter how warm the weather, and no matter how loose you feel, you still need to make sure your arm is fully stretched out. And remember to stretch your legs, too… even if they feel tired from your day with your friends.

As for warm-up pitches, maybe you can throw fewer because the heat is going to take its toll on your energy. You will probably get tired faster, so it's not a bad idea to conserve your efforts.

But remember, that's only if you've stretched out your arms and legs first!

Jon Lester's Memories

I GREW UP south of Seattle, Washington. Baseball season was always a cool time for us because it meant good weather and being outside in the sun.

The main thing about my baseball memories, or sports in general, was just having fun. We didn't play a hundred games when we were twelve years old. We played maybe thirty games and went out and had fun. It didn't matter what sport we were playing. We were kids. We did what we wanted to do when it came to sports, and we didn't get criticized for it. That's probably my biggest memory: being able to play baseball and have fun doing it.

Obviously, I pitched. I also played outfield and a little bit at first base, but not much. I played every game. I was a pretty good hitter. I didn't hit 900 home runs or anything, but I held my own and did fairly well.

It's hard to remember particular games because I played in so many. I'd have two baseball games in the morning and then a basketball game at night. I played as many sports as I could for as long as I could. I enjoyed going to practice and I enjoyed going to the games. Sometimes I'd play baseball in the morning, soccer in the afternoon, and basketball at night.

For me, playing sports was part of growing up. For the most part I was an even-tempered kid. But I think kids go through spurts where they get a little bad-tempered and learn some bad habits. I went through mine for about a year or two, but after that my parents pretty much nipped it in the bud. I think every kid goes through a phase like that. You have your disagreements with refs and umps and teammates—throwing bats and helmets and stuff like that—but in the end, I think playing sports a lot helps you grow out of it.

THE ART OF PITCHING

CC SABATHIA

No two pitchers throw exactly the same way. Their pitching motions might be different, or they might stand on a different place on the **pitching rubber**, or they might use their legs differently. But even though all pitchers throw in their own unique ways, there are some important lessons that every young pitcher should learn.

In this chapter, Cy Young Award–winner CC Sabathia talks about pitching mechanics.

What is *long toss,* and how can it help a pitcher?

Long toss is playing catch at a distance on flat ground, not off a mound.

I might start throwing 60 feet away from the person I'm playing catch with, then move back to 90 feet away and then to 120 feet away.

Probably about twenty to twenty-five throws from each distance is good. Then you continue playing catch, but you start moving closer and closer.

Once you've done that your arm should be nice and loose and you'll be good to go.

Long toss can definitely help you strengthen your arm. I'd say if you start on a long-toss program three days a week—Mondays, Wednesdays, and Fridays, for instance—it will really help you.

In a *windup* position, where do you want to place your foot on the rubber?

As a left-handed pitcher I put my left foot on the rubber.

My foot is so big that I start in the middle of the rubber. I have my foot turned a little bit toward first base when I stand on top of the rubber just so I won't get a lot of extra and unnecessary movement in my **delivery**. When you start your delivery, and you start turning so you can push off the rubber, you have to move that foot to get in the best position to throw a pitch. And I don't want to have to move it too much.

Why can it be a good thing to start with your foot in the middle of the rubber?

I feel you're **squared up** better to the plate that way, but it's something you have to try out. Experiment and see what works best for you.

I've tried putting my foot on both sides of the rubber—to the far left and to the far right. I just kind of ended up in the middle because I'm more comfortable doing it that way, and I've had the best results doing it that way.

Different pitchers start on different places on the rubber. I've watched a lot of pitchers. Left-hander Johan Santana starts on the third-base side of the rubber, but left-hander Jon Lester starts on the first-base side. It all depends on where you're most comfortable.

Does your foot stay on top of the rubber through the entire delivery?

No, it doesn't stay there.

You want to dig a little hole in front of the rubber so when you turn your foot, you can have the outside of your foot resting up against the side of the rubber. That way, you can get a better push-off from the rubber.

Why is a good push-off important?

Driving your legs off the rubber gives you more power. Pitching and getting power in your pitching delivery is not just about using your arm. It's more about using your legs.

You want to make sure when you're pushing off that you stay tall in your delivery, that you don't lean forward or backward, and that you drive down right through the catcher.

Another way of saying "driving down and through the catcher" is the term **follow-through**. For me that means making sure, as I let the ball go, that my hand is in front of my face and that I keep my arm going. I don't want to stop my arm's momentum.

You can look at it this way: for a left-handed pitcher, that means your left hand follows through and keeps on going after you have delivered the ball, so it gets close to your right knee. So think left arm, right knee.

That's what it means when you hear a pitcher talk about "finishing" a pitch—following through with the delivery.

Where are your eyes during your delivery?

I start with my eyes on the **target**, and then as I'm going through the windup I look down, between home plate and first base, because I don't want to be locked in and staring at the target the whole time. But when I get to my **balance point** in my delivery, I look back at the target and keep my eyes on it as I let the ball go.

How important is it to find the target again after you look down?

It's definitely important. Sometimes, if I pick it up too late, the ball will fly on me—sail up and away—say, when I'm facing a right-handed hitter.

Is it okay if your head is moving during the delivery?

Your head should be as still as possible to make sure you know where you're throwing the ball.

How important is it for a pitcher to be balanced in his delivery?

Balance is huge.

When you get to your balance point, you pick up your leg and you're standing tall, not leaning forward or backward, but standing straight and keeping your back leg straight.

15

If you can do that, when you push off and drive down through, it's easier to get a good follow-through and throw strikes.

When you are balanced, should you be able to just stop at that point in your delivery and not fall over?

Uh-huh. That's something you need to practice because it's very important.

When I was a kid we did a drill where we would stop our delivery right there at the balance point and then hop five times forward and five times back. As a left-handed pitcher, I would have picked up my right leg at that point, so I'd be hopping on my left leg. It's the opposite for a right-hander.

That was a good drill. If you fell over, you knew that you weren't balanced.

How important is it to concentrate when you're playing catch and warming up?

Pitching isn't just throwing the ball. You have to practice a lot of different parts of your delivery so your **mechanics** will be right when you're in a game.

When I'm playing long toss or playing catch on flat ground I won't necessarily go through my entire windup, but I'll concentrate on my leg kick and my balance. These exercises for a pitcher are like batting practice for a hitter. It's practice. Aside from throwing in a bullpen, playing long toss and catch are the only times you get to go out there and work on things. After you have played long toss and you come in to throw off the mound, then you can start to concentrate on throwing strikes and throwing the ball to spots on different sides of the plate.

Any time you're throwing the ball as a pitcher, whether you're long-tossing or throwing off the mound before a game, you should be concentrating on what you need to work on.

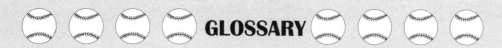 **GLOSSARY**

Balance point: The point during the delivery when a pitcher is balanced with all his momentum gathered to then make a strong pitch to the plate.

Delivery: The act of throwing the ball to the plate.

Follow-through: Completing an arm movement after throwing a pitch.

Long toss: Playing catch at a long distance.

Mechanics: The body movements involved in playing baseball.

Pitching rubber: The rectangular slab in the middle of the pitcher's mound where the pitcher stands.

Squaring up: Turning to face the target.

Target: Where you want to throw the ball.

Windup: The pitcher's motion when there are no runners on base. One or both feet are on the rubber and he faces the hitter head-on as he begins his delivery.

Blown Away!

Stu Miller was not the biggest pitcher in baseball history.

In fact, he stood a shade under six feet tall and weighed only 165 pounds. He was a relief pitcher in the major leagues for sixteen seasons.

In 1961, the right-handed Miller was pitching so well for the San Francisco Giants that he was named to the National League's All-Star team for the first of two All-Star Games that year.

The date was July 11 and the game was being played at the Giants' home field, Candlestick Park.

It was always windy at Candlestick Park. Very windy. And on this particular day, the wind was unusually strong.

Miller entered the game at the top of the ninth inning. But as he began his windup to throw a pitch, a huge gust of wind literally blew him off the pitching rubber. He had to stop his motion to keep from falling over!

While that must have been a rather embarrassing moment for Stu Miller, he soon wound up claiming a more favorable All-Star distinction. Miller was the winning pitcher in the National League's 5–4 victory over the American League.

★★★★★★★★★★★★★★★★★★★★★★★★★★

HERE'S THE SITUATION

The bases are loaded. The game is tied. It's the bottom of the final inning. There are two outs.

The batter coming to the plate is a good hitter.

Should you "nibble" with your pitches, and try to throw a strike over the outside corner of the plate? Or should you throw the ball over the middle and just see what happens?

HERE'S THE SOLUTION

There is no good option in this case.

If you try to throw the first couple of pitches over the corner and you miss, you're down in the count at two balls and no strikes. Now you're in danger of walking in the winning run. No one wants to lose on a bases-loaded walk. So in this case, it's probably better to throw the ball over the plate, even if it's down the middle.

If you make the batter hit the ball, one of your fielders has the chance to make a play. You just might get the batter to ground out to one of your infielders, or hit a lazy fly ball to the outfield. Then you're headed for extra innings and your team can still win the game.

So instead of nibbling, challenge the hitter. Make the batter hit the ball to beat you.

CC Sabathia's Memories

I GREW UP in Vallejo, California. I was a power-hitting first baseman. I didn't pitch a lot, just a little bit.

I just remember baseball being so much fun. When I was twelve our all-star team was pretty good. We almost went to the Little League World Series.

My dad coached me back then. That was good and bad. It was definitely good because it brought us closer and made our relationship tighter, but there were times when it was hard. Sometimes late at night, when he had videotapes of our games and he had me watching my swing to see what I wasn't doing right, it could get a little tough.

I was a left-handed hitter. I hit a bunch of home runs as a kid. I guess the best ones would have to be a grand slam I hit in my last regular-season game as a Little Leaguer, and then a grand slam I hit in the first game in the All-Stars. I also threw a shutout in that first All-Star game, so I had a pretty good day. My dad was pretty happy that day.

Usually after big games we'd go to Mountain Mike's, a pizza parlor in Vallejo. Round Table was another place we went to all the time. My team was Foster Lumber. Three of my cousins were on the team. We had a really, really good team.

I was 5'7" or 5'8". I guess that was pretty big for a twelve-year-old. I always threw hard and I always threw strikes. I didn't throw a breaking ball because I just didn't have one back then. I threw fastballs.

What was more fun, pitching or hitting? For me it definitely was hitting. To this day I still love hitting. I hit sixth in the batting order when I was ten, I hit second when I was eleven, and I hit third when I was twelve. How I remember that, I don't know, but that's what I did. We had some good teams. We won our league three years in a row in the Vallejo Little League.

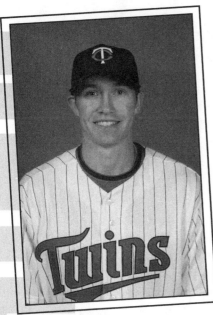

FIELDING
THE POSITION

SCOTT
BAKER

Throwing the ball is only one part of a pitcher's job. He also has to become a fielder when the batter hits the ball in his direction. No matter how good a pitcher is, players will hit at least some of his pitches—and he must be ready to field the ball just like any other fielder.

In this chapter, Scott Baker discusses techniques for becoming a successful fielding pitcher.

How important is it for a pitcher to be a good fielder?

It is very important. Obviously your main job is to pitch well enough to get the hitter out, but you do yourself a favor by also being that ninth fielder.

You always want to start out with a good pitch. You need to focus on getting a strong finish to your pitching motion so you'll be ready to field if the batter gets a hit. As soon as you've thrown the ball, get into a good fielding position so you can react to whatever happens.

What is a good fielding position for a pitcher?

If you look at some of the great fielding pitchers, like Kenny Rogers and Greg Maddux, you'll notice that they end each pitch in a squared-up position, facing the hitter. From this position, a pitcher is ready to field the ball.

Is that easy to do?

It's very difficult to do. You see a lot of pitchers fall off to one side of the mound or the other after they deliver a pitch because they're putting so much effort into the pitch, trying to do whatever they can to get that hitter out. That effort can carry the body to one side.

So a lot of times pitchers are not able to stay lined up to the hitter, facing the plate. When pitchers aren't squared up to the plate, it is harder for them to field a **comebacker**.

How can you get better at ending up in a good fielding position after delivering the pitch?

This is something you have to work at really hard. You want to become better at it because you're not doing yourself justice if you're not able to field a ground ball.

That's why we work on this aspect of the game so much in spring training. We pitchers have a lot of fielding drills, with coaches hitting us ground balls.

What does a pitcher have to do on a ground ball hit to the right side of the infield?

You have to cover first base. Your first movement on a ball hit to the right side is to run toward first base. You do this regardless of whether

23

the first baseman can get the ball and make the play himself or the second baseman has to field it. You have to start heading to first in case either player needs to throw the ball to you at the base for the out.

You don't want to forget to go over there because if no one is covering first, the runner will be safe and you'd be giving the other team an extra out. That happened to me once. I delayed just a little bit and the runner was safe.

So your first movement is toward first base. For the most part, you want to run directly to the base, maybe getting a step or two up the **baseline** from the bag before turning and running on the inside of the baseline to get to first base. That way you can catch the ball, tag the inside of the base, and avoid being stepped on by the runner.

How is fielding a ball as a pitcher different from the way another infielder might field a ball?

There's not much difference. There are certain things you have to do to get the ball to first base regardless of where you're playing in the infield.

After you've fielded the ball, you want to make sure you set your feet and make a good throw to the first baseman. There are certain plays that are a little different, though, like bunt plays.

How do you field a bunt?

The rule of thumb is that if the ball is still rolling when you go to field it, you should pick it up with your glove and your bare hand together. If the ball has stopped rolling, you use your bare hand to pick it up.

What do you do with the ball after you have fielded a bunt?

How you play the bunt depends on the situation. There are different ways to handle bunts.

If there are runners at first and second and you're trying to get the guy out at third base, the third baseman might not charge in for the bunt. So the pitcher may need to go toward third base to cover that area after delivering the pitch. If there's a runner at first and the third baseman and the first baseman are both charging, the pitcher will just charge straight in.

But the really important thing after fielding the ball is to take your time with your throw.

Why do you not want to rush your throw?

Because if you do, you might make a bad throw. You don't want to throw the ball away and put an extra runner in scoring position. If you know the runner has speed, you want to be quick. But you also want to be under control.

A lot of times you tend to want to rush your throw and get it to the base faster than it needs to be there. When you get in too big a hurry, it is tougher to make an accurate throw because your feet aren't set and you're not facing your **target**.

What kind of throw do you make after fielding the ball?

Some position players can make a "flip" kind of throw—not a real **underhand** throw, but just flipping it over to first base with a flick of the wrist. Pitchers, though, have to have good mechanics: they need to set their feet, get on top of the ball, and make a good throw.

As a pitcher, you want to be squared up, with your front shoulder pointing to the target.

After fielding a bunt, what should you do to get a forceout at second base?

That tends to be a longer throw for a pitcher, especially if you're crashing toward home plate to get the ball. You have to be quick. If it's rolling, you pick it up with your glove and your bare hand, then turn quickly toward second base, set your feet, and throw.

Does the second baseman or the shortstop have to be standing on the second-base bag when you make your throw?

You definitely want to be able to pick up whoever is covering the bag in your field of vision to see if he's close to the bag. If you see him getting close to the bag, it's okay to release the ball before he gets there. But you're not going to throw to an uncovered bag.

Where are you aiming your throw at second base?

You want to try to hit whoever is covering the bag in the chest with the throw.

The chances are you're only going to get one out on the play and not a double play, so concentrate on that first out. You want to make an on-target throw to the fielder so he can stretch toward the ball—like a first baseman does—catch it cleanly, and then get the runner. If you aim for the fielder's chest, he'll be able to stretch as far as he needs to.

If there's a runner on first, how do you know which base to throw to after fielding a ball?

The catcher will call out what to do because when you field the ball your back is to second base. If he calls "second," that means he thinks you can get the out at second base, so you turn and throw to second base. If he calls "first," that means you don't have the out at second, so you throw to first base.

On a routine bouncer back to the mound with no one on base, how do you make the play?

After fielding the ball, you want to set your feet, take a little **crow hop** to keep the feet moving so you're not throwing flat-footed, and then throw to first. Again, you want to try to hit the first baseman in the chest with your throw.

What type of throw do you make on a routine bouncer with no one on base if you field the ball between the mound and first base?

On that type of play, you can make an underhand toss. It's just a nice and easy toss, not too hard, because your momentum is bringing you toward first base. That's the easiest type of throw to make on a ball when it's hit like that.

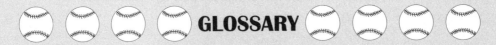 **GLOSSARY**

Baseline: The foul line that extends from home plate to first base.

Comebacker: A ground ball back to the mound.

Crow hop: A quick three-part move used to get into throwing position after fielding a ground ball. The right-handed player takes a quick hop onto the right foot, then strides forward with the left, following through with a right-handed throw.

Spot: The target.

Target: Where you want to throw the ball.

Underhand: A throwing motion in which the palm of the hand faces up toward the sky. Generally a soft, but firm, toss.

An Unusual Toss!

Many pitchers can throw the ball at ninety miles per hour or faster. And there are times when a batter will hit the ball back to the pitcher even faster than that. The pitcher's job is to flag down these missiles. If the ball is hit on the ground, the pitcher has to grab it and throw to first base. This is usually not too difficult, especially if a ball is hit softly. But one day, Orlando "El Duque" Hernandez of the New York Yankees got one of those fast missiles and it caused a slight problem.

Right-hander El Duque was pitching against the New York Mets on June 5, 1999, at Yankee Stadium. He was facing Rey Ordonez, who hit a bouncer toward him. El Duque reached out with his glove and caught the bouncer. The ball settled in the webbing of his glove. The pitcher's momentum took him toward first base. He took a few short, easy strides toward the bag and reached into his glove for the ball. But the ball was stuck in the webbing. It was stuck so tightly El Duque was afraid he wouldn't be able to get the ball out in time to throw to first before Ordonez reached the bag.

So the pitcher did some fast thinking.

He yanked the glove off his left hand and tossed the glove, which still held the baseball, to his first baseman, Tino Martinez. A surprised Martinez caught the glove. Since the ball was secure inside the glove, and since the glove arrived before Ordonez did, Ordonez was called out.

It was just your basic pitcher-to-first-baseman ground ball out, if you were scoring the play. But credit El Duque with some quick, creative problem-solving skills in order to get the out!

★ ★

HERE'S THE SITUATION

The bases are loaded. You're pitching and your team is ahead by one run. It's the last inning. There's only one out. A ground ball is hit back to you at the mound. You field it cleanly.

Should you turn to throw to second base to start a double play? Or should you throw home to stop the tying run from scoring?

HERE'S THE SOLUTION

Go home!

If you throw to second base and you're not able to turn the double play, the tying run will score. Yes, you might be able to get the double play, but it's by no means a sure thing.

The throw home is much more of a sure thing. If you make a good throw and the catcher steps on home plate, you have the forceout. The tying run has not scored. Now you have two outs and you still have a forceout possibility at every base. Plus, if everything goes smoothly, the catcher might have time to throw to first base for a potential game-ending double play.

Scott Baker's Memories

I PLAYED Little League in Shreveport, Louisiana, on a team called the Mets.

I pitched but I also played other positions. I think it's important to play as many positions as possible when you're young so you can figure out where you're most comfortable playing. If you enjoy the game itself, any position that's part of the game is going to be exciting. Some guys might not think it's so great to play the outfield, but everyone has different abilities and some players do well in outfield positions. I played a lot of middle infield, shortstop, and second base. I made the All-Star team every year.

Luckily for me, I had very good coaching from coaches who cared about how we performed. We really practiced quite a bit, which is not something you tend to appreciate until later in life. We had a good group of guys. We went undefeated for two years in a row. But winning or losing wasn't the most important thing. It was just a lot of fun.

Even though I'm a pitcher now, I enjoyed playing other positions and I also liked hitting. I wasn't a real home-run hitter. I hit a few, but I matured late. I wasn't one of the bigger kids. I wasn't real strong. I was more of a singles and doubles hitter. I did always have a good arm, though, one of the better arms in the league.

Where I played, pitchers weren't allowed to throw breaking balls. Our coaches taught us how to hit **spots** with our pitches. If you can throw your fastball and changeup and hit spots, that's going to make you a better pitcher. They taught us good mechanics that allowed you have a repeatable delivery.

I do remember one game when I was eleven years old and I was playing with a lot of kids who were a year older. I usually got plenty of playing time, but on that day, because we were playing a pretty good team and it was a big game, I was sitting on the bench. Our shortstop wasn't doing well, so the coach put me in to play shortstop in the last or the next-to-last inning. On the first play hit to me I turned an unassisted double play. From then on I played shortstop on that team. I remember people being impressed I could make that play. It was a big confidence boost for me. That's a vivid memory.

Scott Blue

THROWING OUT BASESTEALERS

GEOVANY SOTO

The pitch is thrown and the runner on first base takes off for second. He is trying to steal the base. The catcher gets the ball and throws to second to try to nail the runner. But it takes more than just a strong arm to strike down an enemy basestealer.

In this chapter, National League Rookie of the Year and All-Star Geovany Soto talks about the skills that are needed to throw out basestealers.

When you're catching with no one on base, what is your normal *stance*?

Everybody's different, but most of all you want to be comfortable in your stance. You don't want to be tensed up. You want to be relaxed, with your upper body bent over the top of your knees. My right hand is my throwing hand, and I'll put that hand behind my right calf so I can protect that hand from **foul tips**.

The elbow of your catching hand should be outside your knee. You don't want your elbow inside your knee—if you have to move your glove to catch an inside pitch to a right-handed batter, your elbow might bang against your knee and keep you from catching the ball. And you'll still be able to reach the outside pitch to a right-handed batter if your elbow is outside your left knee. If that happens you might not be able to catch it.

When there's a runner on base, and you suspect he might try to steal a base, does anything change with stance?

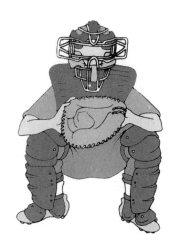

In that situation, your body should be a little more upright and your legs a little more spread out, maybe shoulder width. Your butt should be up a little bit. Your legs should make an "L" with your thighs, like you're sitting on a stool.

Why would you make those changes in your stance?

It's a more powerful position that allows you to catch the ball and throw it. You can be more aggressive.

If you think a runner might steal, do you change the position of your throwing hand?

Yes, you do. Your throwing hand should be made into a fist. You put it right behind your mitt when you give the target and get ready to receive the ball. Your thumb should be inside your fist. But your hand can't be tensed up because if there's a foul tip, it could break a bone. Your hand should be kind of loose and wobbly behind your mitt.

How do you set your feet in your stance when you think a runner might steal second?

If you're right-handed, your left foot should be slightly ahead of your right foot because you want to be in position to throw to second as soon as you catch the ball. You don't want to have your left shoulder pointed directly at second base, though. You still want to be able to give a good **target** to the pitcher. You want to be turned just enough so you can get into your throwing motion quickly when you catch the ball.

Is throwing out basestealers all about having a strong arm?

A strong arm is important, but it's more about getting your body into a smooth rhythm. If you have proper **mechanics**, you won't stress your arm. And remember, your legs are important, too. If you don't have your legs under you in a good, strong, balanced position, when you throw the ball you're going to be getting all of your power only from your arm. If you don't use your legs to push off, eventually you are going to hurt your arm.

How do you get in position to make a quick, strong throw to nail a runner trying to steal second base?

You need to have a proper **transfer**. You have to get the ball from the glove to your throwing hand quickly.

As you're doing that, if you're a right-handed catcher, your left leg goes forward a little bit and turns your body so your toes are pointed to second base. Your front foot should be near the back point of home plate, maybe a little bit to the right of that point.

Your shoulders should be **squared up** to second base. Your left shoulder should be pointing at second base.

When do your feet start to move when you see out of the corner of your eye that a runner is trying to steal?

The split-second before the ball hits your mitt, that's when you start moving.

You can't start too early because then you'll be coming up out of your stance and you won't let the umpire see the pitch to call it a ball or a strike. But in the split-second before the ball hits your mitt, your shoulder should be moving to get into position to point to second base.

It's like a *bang-bang* kind of quick movement. While you're squaring your shoulders up to face second base, your feet are getting into the throwing position.

You want to do it quickly, but you don't want to get off balance and lose control. Keep some of your body weight on your back side—maybe 60 percent on your back side and 40 percent on the left leg—because that's where you get all your power for the throw as you push off.

Why do you want your left shoulder pointing toward second base in this instance?

If your left shoulder is pointing, say, where the shortstop usually stands, then your body is opening up and will not be in a direct line with the base you're throwing to. When you open up like that, it will cause your throw to **tail** and sink, because you won't be on top of the ball. You'll be throwing with more of a sidearm motion and that will make your throw less accurate. You should be aiming at second base with your shoulder for a more accurate throw.

What is the best *arm angle* to throw out a basestealer?

Everybody's a little different, but catchers seem to throw from behind the ear. If you're right-handed, your right hand would come up by your right ear when you throw.

Catchers don't have a long motion when they throw. They just catch the ball and throw it. It should almost be like an "L," with the arm out straight to the right from the shoulder (for a right-hander) and the elbow bent in a 90-degree angle. Catchers don't reach back when we throw. We have to be as quick as we can at catching the ball and throwing it to second base.

There are a lot of movements for a catcher to throw out a basestealer. But the key is being in a rhythm. Slow stuff down in your mind so all your mechanics are good. Better mechanics will get you a better time to second.

How do you grip the ball?

You want to have a **four-seam grip** on the ball. That way the ball won't move anywhere after you throw it. It's not going to sink, it's not going to cut. It's going to go straight and it's going to go through the bag.

Where do you want to aim your throw?

You don't want to throw a ball so it just reaches the front of the bag. You want to throw it through the bag. That's the most important thing.

You want to make a hard throw like you're throwing to the belt of the player covering the bag—the shortstop or the second baseman. That will give the ball the best carry it can have. The fielder will be squatting down a bit to get the ball, so if you aim right to the belt it will be a perfect throw for a tag at second base.

Are the mechanics of trying to throw out a basestealer at third base any different from throwing to second base?

You want to use the same mechanics, but you don't have to turn your body as much because your left shoulder is already kind of aiming to third base.

All you have to do is **clear the batter**. After you catch the ball, wait a little longer to make sure your balance is under control because it's a shorter throw—for the most part, the path will be clear for you to throw to third base. So if you're already squared up, it's just a matter of catching the ball while you're transferring it to your throwing arm, taking a small step back, and making the throw.

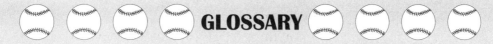 **GLOSSARY**

Arm angle: The position of your arm as you throw the ball.

Clearing the batter: Moving so that the batter is not in the path of a throw to a base.

Foul tip: A ball barely hit by the batter that sometimes strikes the catcher.

Four-hole hitter: The batter who hits fourth, or cleanup, in the lineup; generally the team's most powerful hitter.

Four-seam grip: A grip of the baseball in which the fingers are positioned across, not with, the four seams of the ball. This grip produces a rotation that keeps the ball moving in a straight line.

Mechanics: The body movements involved in playing baseball.

Squaring up: Turning to face the target.

Stance: A player's body position.

Tail: The sideways movement of a ball thrown with a sidearm motion. For a right-handed thrower, the ball will "tail" from left to right as it nears the target.

Target: Where you want to throw the ball.

Transferring: Moving the ball from the glove to the throwing hand.

Heads Up!

On May 12, 1967, the Detroit Tigers' Al Kaline took his lead from first base. Jon Wyatt was pitching for the Red Sox and Bob Tillman was the catcher.

On Wyatt's second pitch to the batter, Kaline broke for second, attempting to steal. Tillman caught the pitch and then fired a throw to second base. Wyatt turned his head toward second base to see what would happen.

But Tillman's throw was low. It smacked Wyatt on the back of the head, knocking the pitcher to the ground. The ball rolled to the on-deck circle between home plate and the first-base dugout. Kaline made it all the way to third base before the ball was picked up.

Fortunately, Wyatt wasn't badly hurt. He had a headache, but he stayed in the game. On the next pitch, the batter hit a sacrifice fly off Wyatt, driving in Kaline for the winning run in the Tigers' 5–4 victory over the Red Sox.

★ ★

HERE'S THE SITUATION

The other team has runners at first and second and there are two outs. The runner at second base has very good speed. But the runner at first base is not very fast at all. The pitch comes in. It's an easy one to catch. Both runners take off. It's a double steal.

As the catcher, you now have to make a decision. Do you throw to third base, trying to get the lead runner? Or do you throw to second base, knowing that the runner from first base doesn't have great speed?

HERE'S THE SOLUTION

Throw to second!

If you get an out, the inning is over. The pitch is an easy one to handle, so you should throw to the base where you have the best chance for success. In this case, it's second base, because the runner from first is slower than the runner from second.

But remember, there's one important thing you have to do as a catcher. You always have to anticipate what might happen. If you think the other team might try a double steal, you must let your infielders know, through a sign, which base you will be throwing to. That way, you'll make sure they cover the bag.

Geovany Soto's Memories

I GREW UP in Puerto Rico and played there between the ages of eight and twelve. We played from February to August. We lived and died for baseball, like we do now. It's more our jobs right now, but back then it was what we lived for. The most important highlight for me was the time my team went to the 1995 American Amateur Baseball Congress World Series when I was twelve years old. The World Series was in Puerto Rico. We played teams from Texas, California, and other places—and we ended up winning. In that World Series, I hit .722. I had fifteen RBI in seven games and I was MVP and batting champion. I was always a **four-hole hitter**, a big home-run guy. I used to be the stud of the team. I had fun.

My dad always encouraged me. He wasn't my coach but he knew a lot. He gave me extra practice at home and was always passionate about the game. We played on a Little League field in Trujillo Alto, which is right next to San Juan, and we would have like a thousand people watching us there. It was intense but it was a nice, fun environment.

42

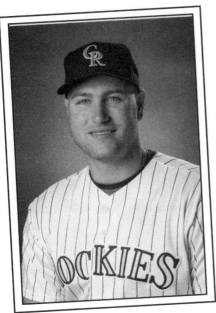

CATCHING FOUL POP-UPS

CHRIS IANNETTA

It looks so easy: The ball is fouled by the batter and it floats high in the air, right around home plate. The catcher has such a big glove. How could he possibly miss it? Well, nothing is ever as easy as it looks…and that goes for foul pop-ups, too.

In this chapter, Chris Iannetta talks about the dos and don'ts of catching foul pop-ups—so you can make sure that what goes up comes down in your mitt!

What is the first thing you do when a batter hits a foul pop-up around the plate?

The first thing is to try and recognize where the ball is going. Then you take the mask off, get a visual of where the ball is, and then try and get yourself in position to catch it.

If the ball is hit directly behind you, does it tend to go straight up and come straight back down?

Usually when a foul ball is popped up right behind home plate, it's going to come back to you as it comes down.

But you actually don't want to position yourself right under the ball in this case because the ball will have **backspin** on it as it comes down. It won't be coming straight back down. The spin will take it toward the field.

If you don't want to get right under this type of foul pop-up, where do you want to position yourself?

You want to keep the ball about four to five feet in front of you as you're tracking it because the ball will come back to you, but you don't want to stop your feet from moving, either. You don't want to be flat-footed. You want to shuffle your feet back and forth a little bit, picking them up and putting them down, staying under control.

You don't want to be moving so much that your eyes are bouncing all over the place because then the ball is going to look like it's bouncing and will be harder to catch. But you do want to keep yourself moving a little because then it will be easier to react to the ball. For instance, if the wind takes the ball somewhere unexpected, you'll be able to judge where it's coming down and move in that direction. It's harder to react and move where you need to go if you are flat-footed and motionless.

How do you run after a pop-up?

You run on the balls of your feet. If you run on your heels it makes your eyes bounce up and down and the ball looks like it's bouncing up and down, too.

Which way are you facing when a foul ball goes up behind you?

You get up out of your **stance** and turn around. You want to keep your back to the field of play at all times because the backspin is going to bring the ball back to you. If you don't turn your back to the field, it's going to be difficult to **read** the ball. If you're facing the field, trying to backpedal to catch the ball, it's going to be coming back over your head and that makes it a much more difficult catch.

What do you do with the mask?

After you take it off, you hold it in your throwing hand. And when the ball gets to its peak, reaches its highest point, that's when you throw the mask as far away from you as you can. You don't want to just drop it near you because if the ball drifts a little bit, you don't want to step on it as you try to catch the ball. If that happens, you might miss the ball and you could get hurt, too.

Don't worry about hitting the umpire or anyone with the mask. They'll be expecting you to throw it, so they should be able to get out of the way.

How do you hold your glove to make the catch?

You want to put your glove hand up like any fielder catching a ball in the air. After you throw the mask, place your throwing hand behind the glove. You want to move your body into a position where the ball will be coming right down on your chin as you're looking up. Line it up so that if you didn't have a glove, the ball would hit you on the chin.

Your glove should be as open as possible.

Why is your bare hand next to the glove?

Catching with two hands helps secure the ball in the glove. If the ball rolls around in the glove or pops out, you can still make the catch with your bare hand.

How much does the wind affect a catcher in making this play?

A big part of being able to catch a foul pop-up is checking the wind and knowing which way it might push the ball. You have the spin of the baseball to worry about, too. If the wind is blowing one way and the spin of the baseball is pushing it the other way, you're facing a difficult play.

You just have to keep **judging it** and watching it all the way, trying to anticipate where the ball will be going and making adjustments to get there.

How do you deal with the sun on a pop-up?

You use your glove or bare hand to shield your eyes and block the sun. You try to navigate around the sun's glare as best you can. It can be a difficult situation.

Do you ever take your eye off the ball when you're tracking a foul pop-up?

The only time you'll take your eye off the ball is if you get close to a fence. You want to check the fence out early, to see how close you are, because later you don't want to have to take your eye off the ball just as you're trying to catch it. You can also put out a hand to get a feel for how close you are getting to the fence without taking your eye off the ball.

How aggressively do you approach trying to catch a pop-up in fair territory?

If it's in fair territory, maybe five to fifteen feet in front of home plate, you still go for it, but on this play it's not the priority of the catcher to make the catch. The third baseman or the first baseman will be making that play. You still track the ball and attack it as if you're going to catch it, but you expect one of them to **call you off**. When you hear them, you do your best to get out of their way.

The catcher is the last priority on this type of ball. The infielders are running in for the ball so they have a better visual on it.

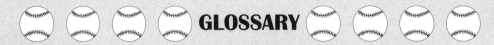# GLOSSARY

Backspin: The backward rotation of a ball.

Calling off: When one fielder thinks he has an easier play on a ball than the other fielders, he will "call off" other teammates who are trying to make the play so he can make the catch himself.

Judging it: Understanding where the ball may come down.

Reading: Another way of saying "judging the ball."

Stance: A player's body position.

Taking a lead: Standing a few steps off the base before the pitcher delivers a pitch.

"Tools of ignorance": A humorous term for catchers' gear that refers to the dangerous and unpleasant aspects of the position.

Petey On The Spot!

The Philadelphia Phillies' first World Series title was so close that the team and their fans at Veterans Stadium could almost taste victory. On October 21, 1980, the Phillies had a three-run lead in the top of the ninth inning. Philadelphia also had a three-games-to-two lead over the Kansas City Royals in the best-of-seven series.

But the Royals began to rally against Philadelphia left-hander Tug McGraw. A one-out walk and then back-to-back singles filled the bases, bringing Frank White to the plate. McGraw threw a pitch, and White lofted it foul. The ball drifted toward the Phillies' dugout, along the first-base line. Philadelphia catcher Bob Boone, one of the best defensive catchers to ever play the game, gave chase. He spotted the ball, tossed aside his mask, and moved over to the dugout in pursuit.

As he did so, first baseman Pete Rose also raced in to give chase. If Boone couldn't get to the ball, Rose must have figured, maybe he'd be in position to grab it. Boone got to the ball and reached out with his mitt. The ball hit his mitt, but Boone didn't catch it cleanly. The ball hopped up into the air and looked as if it would fall to the turf. But Rose was close enough to save the day. He reached out with his glove and plucked the ball out of the air before it hit the ground. The Phillies got the out!

It was the second out of the inning. The Royals still had the bases loaded, but McGraw struck out the next Kansas City hitter, Willie Wilson, for the final out. The Phillies won the game and their first World Championship!

★ ★

HERE'S THE SITUATION

There's a runner at third base and only one out. The batter lifts a high foul pop-up, near the first-base dugout. You quickly rip off your mask, holding it in your hand. You spot the ball and start to run over to the first-base dugout. You toss away your mask, get under the ball, and make the catch.

What do you do next?

HERE'S THE SOLUTION

After you've made the catch, you can't start snoozing. Unless there are three outs, there's always another play to make. In this case, after you've made the catch, the runner at third base could tag up and score. So after making the catch, you must quickly turn and check to see what the runner is doing. If the runner has tagged and is running home, you'll be ready to throw to the plate.

This is where teamwork comes into play. Obviously, you can't cover the plate yourself, because you had to make the catch near the first-base dugout. Either the third baseman or the pitcher should be covering the plate.

Chris Iannetta's Memories

I PLAYED Little League in North Providence, Rhode Island. I was in the farm system at eight and in the Little League at nine.

I think I only got one hit when I was eight and, actually, I think it might have been an error and not really a hit. I hit a pop-up to third base. It went off the third baseman's glove and they gave me a hit.

I played as a third baseman, but when I was ten, the catcher on our team broke his wrist. A friend looked at me and said, "You look like a catcher," and I went back there and put on all the pieces of equipment a catcher has to wear. I was too naïve back then to know they were the **"tools of ignorance."**

My best friend and I would pick guys off at first base. In Little League, you couldn't **take a lead**. You couldn't get off the bag until the ball crossed the plate. So as soon as the ball crossed the plate, the runner would jump off the bag and I'd throw it down to my friend at first and we'd catch the guys off. I used to pitch, too. Pitching was pretty fun. I was a typical pitcher with a fastball and a curveball. A lot of guys were hitting ten or fifteen or twenty home runs, but I only hit four home runs when I was twelve.

After a game we'd go to the snack bar, get a hot dog and a soda. And if we won a big game there'd be a pool party. We won the district championship when I was twelve and went to a coach's house for a pool party.

I always dragged my parents to the field for games, trying to be the first one there. We'd get to the parking lot really early and have to wait five to ten minutes for the next people to arrive. I couldn't stand being late. I always wanted to be there first.

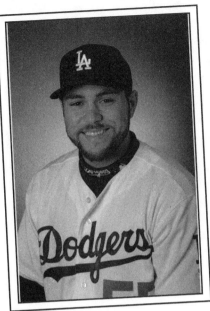

BLOCKING PITCHES IN THE DIRT

RUSSELL MARTIN

There is nothing glamorous about blocking pitches in the dirt. And sometimes it hurts. But as a catcher, you can't let a bad pitch bounce away with runners on base if you can help it.

In this chapter, All-Star Russell Martin discusses the best body position for blocking pitches in the dirt.

What is the first key for a catcher when it comes to blocking a ball in the dirt?

The main thing is being mentally prepared for the ball to go in the dirt. On any given pitch, you have to be expecting the ball to bounce in the dirt. You don't want to be surprised by a ball in the dirt, because you won't be ready to block it.

So there's a mental part to blocking pitches in the dirt, and then the rest is technique—putting your body in the right position to make sure the ball doesn't get past you.

What is the correct body position to make sure a ball doesn't get past you?

First, hold your glove to cover the **"five hole"** because you don't want the ball to go between your legs. The glove would be open, with the palm up, to catch the ball. To protect your bare hand, hold it behind your glove.

In this situation, are you trying to make a clean catch of the ball?

The key isn't so much to catch the ball, but to make sure it doesn't get through you and also to make sure you keep it in front of you. You don't necessarily want to try and catch the ball because sometimes when you do, you'll lift your glove to try to catch the ball, which then might slip underneath the glove and get by you.

What body angle is the best for blocking pitches?

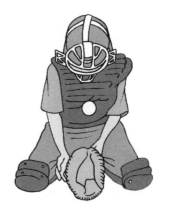

When some guys are going down, they will keep their feet underneath them as they lean forward to block the ball. Some guys will fall forward and let their feet slide out to the side. It doesn't matter, do whatever is more comfortable for you.

I don't know if there's a perfect angle for leaning forward, but you want to make sure to create a body angle that will cause the ball to hit you in the **chest protector** and then fall to the ground in front of you. Whether the ball hits you in the chest or somewhere else, you want it to hit at an angle that makes the ball kind of die in front of you.

What can happen if you don't lean forward?

If you're up too straight, the ball will bounce off you and go too far out in front of you. If that happens, it will be easy for baserunners to advance.

Is your body stiff when you block a pitch?

Not for me.

If your body is stiff while you're blocking a ball, that will make it shoot out away from you after it hits you.

So you have to teach yourself to stay relaxed at the same time you're blocking the ball. It's not easy to do at first. You kind of exhale at the same time you're blocking the ball, almost like you're smothering the ball, catching it with your body.

That's probably the toughest thing to learn, how to absorb the force of the ball as it hits you. But if you can do that, it will **deaden** the ball and cause it to fall right in front of you, and that will keep the baserunners from advancing.

What if a pitch bounces in the dirt and it's to one side or the other? How do you stop that one from getting past you?

I was taught that you **throw your hands** toward where you want the rest of your body to go. You let your hands lead and your body will follow, including your feet. You want to end up in the same good body position as if you were blocking a ball that was coming in dead-on. So throwing your hands out will help your body shift into that position.

Do different types of pitches bounce differently?

Absolutely.

How does that affect you in trying to block the ball?

Sharp **sliders**, for instance, kind of bounce back toward you after they hit the dirt because of the spin on the ball. Let's say there's a right-hander pitching. If he throws a slider heading to the outside corner of the plate to a right-handed hitter, it would hit the dirt and then it would bounce back toward the plate.

That's something you have to **read**. Experience helps. The more pitches like that you see, the better idea you have of where it's going to end up if it's in the dirt. Over time you learn to block balls like that better.

How difficult is it to block a fastball?

With a fastball, you have to be quick enough to get down and block it. It doesn't have to look pretty.

You want your technique to be perfect, but ultimately the goal is just to find a way to knock the ball down and keep it in front of you. Whatever you can do; however you can do it. Sometimes you just have to use your reflexes to stop the ball and get your body in the way. You just have to do whatever you can to make sure the ball doesn't get past you.

How do you get better at blocking pitches?

If you're just starting out, you want to make sure you get as much work as possible. Have someone throw you balls in the dirt so you can get better at blocking them. If you work hard enough at it, at some point it just becomes muscle memory. You want to practice until it becomes a reflex to get in the best body position to block a ball in the dirt.

    GLOSSARY

Chest protector: The piece of the catcher's equipment that protects the chest.

Deadening: Stopping the ball from bouncing or rolling.

"Five hole": The space between the catcher's legs.

Reading: Watching carefully to get an idea of where the ball is going to bounce, how high it might bounce, and what kind of spin it may have when it gets to the fielder.

Slider: A type of pitch that is thrown hard so that it has a small, sharp, late break.

Throwing your hands: Quickly moving your hands toward a target.

One That Got Away!

Not much got past Mickey Owen. He was the best defensive catcher in the National League in 1941, starring for the Brooklyn Dodgers before they moved to Los Angeles. Owen set a league record that year. He handled 476 consecutive chances without an error. Over the course of the season, he compiled a .995 fielding position, which was a Dodgers record. But in the 1941 World Series against the New York Yankees, Owen was unable to hang onto a pitch from Hugh Casey. And that miscue helped the Yanks win the World Championship.

Up until that fateful moment in Game 4 at the Dodgers' Ebbetts Field, it looked as if Brooklyn was on the verge of tying the Series at two games apiece. With two outs in the top of the ninth, Casey and the Dodgers were one strike away from a 4–3 win. But the pitch that Casey threw to Tommy Henrich dipped away from Owen.

He couldn't catch strike three.

The ball got past him, and Henrich made it safely to first base.

The Yankees promptly made Owen and the Dodgers pay for the extra out. New York scored four runs after the miscue and won the game, 7–4. That gave the Yankees a 3–1 lead in the series, and the next day, New York notched the Series-clinching victory by a 3–1 score.

The Dodgers didn't make it back to the World Series until 1947, and didn't win a World Championship until 1955, in their eighth Series appearance.

★★★★★★★★★★★★★★★★★★★★★★★★★★★★★★★

HERE'S THE SITUATION

Runners are at first and third, with two outs. Your team is ahead by one run in the last inning. The pitcher delivers a ball in the dirt. You manage to block it. The ball doesn't get past you, but it squirts away a few feet in front of you. You scramble and quickly retrieve the ball. The runner at third starts down the line. But he sees the ball is still in front of you, so he decides to head back toward third.

The runner at first takes off for second base when the ball bounces away from you. Should you try to throw him out at second?

HERE'S THE SOLUTION

Many thoughts might be passing through your mind as you grab the ball and look up to see what's happening. How fast is the runner moving toward second base? Is an infielder covering second? How good a grip do you have on the ball? How far down the third-base line is the runner from third? If you throw to second, will the runner from third break for home?

There's only one way you should make the throw to second in this case: if you are 100 percent positive that you can throw the runner out at second base. If you're not 100 percent certain, then hold onto the baseball. Don't throw it. You'll still be up one run, and you're still one pitch away from winning the game.

Now, if you were ahead by six runs and there were two outs in the final inning, you might take a shot at throwing out the runner trying for second. If it doesn't work, and the runner from third scores on the play, it's not that big a deal… you're still up five runs. But with two outs in a close game, it's not worth the risk.

Russell Martin's Memories

I GREW UP in Montreal. When I was eight to twelve my dad was my coach. I pretty much played every position. I caught a little bit, but mainly I played shortstop and center field and pitched.

In Canada we have Little League, PeeWee, Bantam, and Midget. That's what the levels are called. Same thing as hockey.

I especially remember the tournament games. One that comes to mind was when I was on an all-star team. I was about twelve years old, playing against all the best players from all the big cities in the province of Quebec, where I was from.

The all-star coach that year had a rule that everybody on the team had to play. I was one of the best players on the team, and he decided I wasn't going to play the first game. Being the competitor that I am, I wasn't too happy about that decision, but I didn't really show it to anyone. I just bit the bullet and watched the game.

It was a tie game in the fifth or sixth inning, and it started raining and got postponed to the next day. After a few more innings, it was still a tie game, and the coach still hadn't put me in.

I almost had tears in my eyes because I wanted to play so badly. Finally the coach's son went up to his dad and said, "I want Russell to play. He really wants to get in there."

With the intensity I had, I just wanted to get in there and I wanted to win the game. Then when there were two outs, the coach's son was supposed to go up to hit. But the coach came to me and said, "Go get a bat, get your helmet."

The relief and the joy I felt were incredible. So I went up to the plate. There was no one on base. It was the bottom of the tenth inning, a long game since we normally only played six innings. Of course, I was hoping for a homer. I worked the count to 3 and 2, and I hit a home run. We won the game.

That was a good trip around the bases. It felt like I was floating. That's one of my best memories as a kid growing up playing baseball.

It was a great time.

FIRST BASE

MARK TEIXEIRA

The first baseman is usually very active during the course of a game. He makes throws. He fields ground balls. He catches throws from other infielders. Occasionally, he has to field bunts or line drives and participate in double-play situations.

In this chapter, All-Star Mark Teixeira talks about what it takes to play a strong first base.

What is the normal fielding position for a first baseman?

Your legs are bent, your butt is down, and your hands are out in front of you, a little bit above the ground. That's the best position to be in.

You want to make sure you're low to the ground so you can field a ground ball. You want your hands out so you can actually catch the ball. If the ball should take a **bad hop** on you, it's much easier to react when your hands are out. Always start with your hands out and move them in to react and catch the ball. When you start with your hands in really close to your body it's a lot harder to react to the ball, especially if it takes a bad hop. If you misread a hop, sometimes the ball hits you.

Is fielding a grounder for a first baseman any different from fielding a grounder at another infield position?

The only difference is that you have more time as a first baseman because you're usually just concerned with catching the ball. You generally don't have to worry about getting yourself into position to throw the ball right after you catch it.

You make very few throws from first base, so your main task is usually to catch the ball and then run over to first base to step on the bag.

If it looks as if it's going to be hard to catch a ball, you can get in front and block it. You try not to block the ball with just your body, though. You want to use your glove.

Should you always get in front of the ball?

Definitely, no matter what position you're fielding, you always want to be in front of the ball when you can.

What are the mechanics of making a throw to second base after fielding a ground ball?

There are two ways to do it.

After fielding the ball, you can do a full spin and throw that way. That means turning toward the outside. You actually turn your back to second base and you spin around toward right field and throw as you come around and **pick up** second base. To second base it's actually easier to spin because it's such a long throw.

The other way is to **pivot** so your body always stays toward second base and you throw **sidearm**.

Why throw sidearm?

Because it's almost impossible to throw from **over the top** as you're pivoting across your body to make the throw.

Aren't you worried the throw won't be as accurate if you throw sidearm?

Well, the ball will **tail** a little bit, so you actually have to play the tail, expecting it to move in that direction. You aim the throw so that when it tails the throw still gets to the base.

If there's someone running from first to second on such a play, how does that affect the way you make this play?

You want to make sure you have plenty of room between the path of the ball and the runner because you don't want to hit the runner in the helmet or in the back with the ball. If that happens, the runner will be safe.

What do you do when a ground ball is not hit to you?

You run straight to first base. No matter where the ground ball is. If you can't field it, you have to go straight to first base to get ready for the throw from whichever player fields the ball.

What are you looking at when you're running to cover the bag? The ground ball? The base?

I really just look at the bag to make sure I'm going right toward it. And once I get to the bag, I pick up wherever the ball was hit and I make sure I give the fielder a good **target** to throw to.

Where do you want to put your foot when you get to the bag?

I put my foot on the inside part, the side facing the second-base bag.

I'm a left-handed catcher, with the glove on my left hand. I put my right heel up against the bag, barely touching it, with my left foot extended toward the infielder who will be making the throw. I reach out with my left hand, my glove hand, to catch the ball. This foot position is generally best for right-handed catchers, too.

Why don't you put your foot on the very top of the base?

Because the runner is running down the first-base line. If you put your foot on top of the base, the runner might step on your foot. If that happens either you or the runner can get hurt.

Do you always put your right foot on the bag when you're catching a throw from a fielder?

The only time I switch feet is on a ball that is fielded by the catcher or the pitcher. That's when I will put my left foot on the bag. This position gives them a big target to throw to on the inside of the baseline in fair territory, and the throw won't come close to hitting the runner.

As a right-handed thrower, does it help to have your right foot on the bag instead of the left?

No matter how you're catching, right-handed or left-handed, you always want to have your right foot on the bag in normal circumstances and your left leg out front. If you have your left foot on the bag, you can't stretch out as far, especially to your right side for a wide throw.

Do you stretch for the ball right away?

No, if you stretch out too early, it will take you more time to change directions. You wait until the ball is thrown so you can see where it's going. Once you know where the ball is going, then you can stretch out in the correct direction and reach toward the ball.

What are the techniques for scooping a throw in the dirt?

You have to keep your glove low to the ground. Once you see where the ball is going and you can tell where it's going to hop up, then you take the glove low and scoop it along the ground and then upwards to catch the ball.

It's almost always a **backhand** catch. Every now and then you have to scoop forehand, but it's easier to scoop backhand because your glove is in a better position and you have more coverage. You want to scoop a throw in the dirt backhand as often as possible.

How can you tell where the ball is going to go when it hits the dirt?

It takes a long time to learn how to **read** the ball. Practice is the key. It's not easy to read exactly where a ball is going to go, especially because grass and dirt conditions vary from field to field. But you hope it's a close-enough scoop so you can **short-hop** it. A short hop is always preferred because it's a little easier to handle.

Where are your hands when you scoop a ball?

They are always out away from you because you want them as close to the ball as possible.

How does a first baseman play a bunt?

As soon as you see the batter **square** you have to run toward the batter because that ball might be bunted near you. The second base-man should be covering the first-base bag. So if the bunt is along the first-base line, you pick up the ball and make a good throw to the second baseman.

Do you spin around to make this throw after fielding the bunt?

No, you just go forward and field the ball. Then you immediately take one step turning yourself toward first base and throw to the player covering first. And when you throw the ball to first, you want to aim your throw to the inside of the bag, in fair territory, because you never want to hit the runner going down the baseline.

# GLOSSARY

Backhand: Reaching across with the glove over to the bare-handed side of the body.

Bad hop: A ball that doesn't bounce in a predictable manner. It may bounce unexpectedly to the left or right or even up high.

Inside-the-parkers: Home runs that do not go over a fence. The batted ball stays in the field of play as the hitter circles the bases.

Over the top/Overhand: A throwing motion in which the arm comes up close to and past the ear when releasing the ball.

Picking up: Looking for and finding a particular target.

Pivoting: Turning or twisting your body.

Reading: Watching carefully to get an idea of where the ball is going to bounce, how high it might bounce, and what kind of spin it may have when it gets to the fielder.

Short hop: A bounce close to the fielder. It is just enough out of reach so that he can't catch the ball with his glove before it hits the ground.

Sidearm: A throwing motion in which the arm is about waist-high and parallel to the ground upon release of the ball.

Squaring up: Turning to face the target.

Tail: The sideways movement of a ball thrown with a sidearm motion. For a right-handed thrower, the ball will "tail" from left to right as it nears the target.

Target: Where you want to throw the ball.

A Lapse at First That Was Second to None

Bill Buckner was a very good player. He hit the ball well and was a solid first baseman. Above all, he was a warrior—someone who played hard despite painful injuries. Buckner had bad ankles that required medical treatment before and after each game. He was a guy you'd always want to have on your team.

Unfortunately for Bill Buckner, though, he will forever be remembered for one play he didn't make: a ground ball hit by the New York Mets player Mookie Wilson against the Boston Red Sox in Game 6 of the 1986 World Series. Buckner's misplay in the tenth inning came in full view of 55,078 fans at Shea Stadium, as well as a national television audience. And it came after the Red Sox had squandered a chance to win their first World Series title since 1918.

Boston was leading the best-of-seven Series, three games to two. The Red Sox had broken a tie and taken a 5–3 lead in the top of the tenth inning. All that was standing in the way of the Sox and their long-coveted World Championship was three outs in the bottom of the tenth. And their reliever, Calvin Schiraldi, got the first two batters out.

With one out left in the game, Gary Carter singled. So did Kevin Mitchell. And then Ray Knight singled, driving in Carter and sending Mitchell to third base. The next batter, Mookie Wilson, watched a wild pitch from Bob Stanley come flying past him and the catcher Rich Gedman. This allowed Mitchell to score the tying run. Then, on a 3–2 pitch, Wilson hit a slow roller down the first-base line. Buckner moved over to his left to field the ball. But he didn't get his glove down low enough. The ball rolled between Buckner's legs and into right field for an error. Knight scored easily, giving the Mets an amazing 6–5 win that tied the World Series at three games apiece.

In Game 7, the Red Sox coughed up an early three-run lead in an 8–5 loss as the New York Mets captured the World Championship.

HERE'S THE SITUATION

You're playing first base. There's a runner at first and one out. The batter hits a ground ball toward the line, not far from the first-base bag. You move to your left and grab the grounder. You know you want to get the double play. But when you field the grounder, you're not sure what to do.

Should you tag the first-base bag and then throw to second base? Or should you spin around and throw to second base and then rush back to cover first for the return throw?

HERE'S THE SOLUTION

You have to make a quick decision. If you're more than a couple of steps from the bag, your best option is to spin around and make the throw to second for the forceout. That way, if you don't end up getting the second out at first base, at least you've cut down the lead runner. And if the ball is relayed back to you in time, then you have your double play. But if you feel your body's momentum is taking you toward first base as you field the ball, it's better to step on the bag for the first out and then throw to second, where the fielder would have to tag the runner for the second out on the play. If the first baseman steps on the bag for the first out, the force at second base is removed, making it necessary to tag the runner for the second out of the double play.

Mark Teixeira's Memories

I GREW UP in Severna Park, Maryland, and played baseball since I was a little kid. I played on a lot of spring and summer teams when I was between eight and twelve and had a lot of great times. We were always the Severna Park Green Hornets.

I played shortstop mostly. I was a good hitter. I loved switch-hitting, but I didn't start doing it full-time until I was thirteen. I did a little bit of switch-hitting in Little League. If it was a blowout or a practice game I would hit left-handed.

I was a natural right-handed hitter, but I always kind of messed around with batting left-handed. My dad wanted to give me a challenge—he told me to try taking batting practice left-handed, and I did. It worked out well for me.

Probably my first home run stands out. I might have been ten or eleven. As a kid your home runs are usually **inside-the-parkers**, where you just run forever. But the first time I hit the ball over the fence was pretty neat. I remember it was right-handed and it was straight down the left-field line.

I pitched, too, but not that much. My dad never let me throw a curveball because he didn't want me to hurt my arm throwing curveballs at a young age. So I actually had kind of a split-finger changeup type of pitch that I would use in addition to my fastball. You really need to learn how to throw a fastball at that age and not worry about throwing other pitches.

The best part of playing shortstop is that a lot of balls are hit to you. You're always in the game, turning double plays. I loved it over there.

I remember when we were real young we got stars on our hats for good plays or for winning a game. The postgame sno-cones were always big, too. I was a big fan of grape sno-cones.

Mark Tei

SECOND BASE

AKINORI IWAMURA

The second baseman doesn't have to make many long throws. Usually, he only has to make a nice and easy throw. But that doesn't mean he never has tough plays to make—plays that require agility and arm strength.

In this chapter, Akinori Iwamura talks about how to make the routine—and not-so-routine—play at second base.

What are the basic mechanics for catching a ground ball as a second baseman?

Get in front of the ball, and concentrate on catching the ball first. Unless you catch the ball, you cannot throw it to first base for the out. So getting it firmly into your glove is the most important thing.

Where should the glove be when you are in the process of catching a ground ball?

If the ground ball is strong, you want to catch it in the middle of your glove. The ideal position is to have your glove at an angle approaching 90 degrees to the ground, not flat on the ground. It's hard to get to 90 degrees, but you want to be as close to that as you can, with the glove tilted up so the ball goes into the middle of the glove and not against the heel.

Where do you have your bare hand when you're fielding a grounder?

You put your bare hand right by the glove and catch the ball with both hands. Think about an alligator's mouth: your bare hand is the top of the mouth closing down over your glove.

You want to have your bare hand close to the glove because the most important thing after you catch the ball is to get rid of the ball. You want to throw the ball as quickly as possible.

What if it's a hard ground ball? How close to the glove should you put your bare hand?

If it's a hard ground ball, you could injure your bare hand if it's too close to the glove, so get your bare hand a little away from the glove. But if it's a weak ground ball, put your bare hand right by the glove.

How close to your body are your glove and bare hand when you are catching a ground ball?

You don't want your hands in too close to your body because then it's difficult to see the ball go into the glove. If your eye angle is looking straight down as the ball is going into the glove, that's not too good. You have to make sure you look at the ball from kind of a far angle, so you want your hands out a bit from the body when you're getting the ground ball.

What are you watching as the ball comes to you on the ground?

You're looking at the ball. You have to be able to anticipate and observe the ball, **reading** the first **hop** and then the second hop, seeing how fast it is moving. Then you might catch it on the third hop. However the ball is hit to you, you have to practice reading the spin on the ball to know how it's going to hop. That way you know whether you have to come in on the ball or stay back on it.

What are the mechanics for making a throw after catching a routine ground ball?

One of the most important things is to know your distance from first base when you catch the ball. Know exactly where you are on the field.

If you're far from first base and you throw softly, you cannot get the runner out. And if you're close and you throw too hard, it's going to be an error because it's going to be difficult for the first baseman to handle and he might not catch it.

How do you make a *backhand* play, catching a ground ball to your right?

Basically you make sure your glove is open as you reach for the ball. A lot of times when players are reaching for the ball, the pinkie finger on the glove hand is closed a little, and if that's the case, you cannot catch the ball in the middle part of the glove, because the glove won't be open wide enough. So make sure it is open.

If you are right-handed with the glove on your left hand and you catch the ball on your right side, your distance for a throw to first base is usually farther than when you catch a ball in front of you. So you have to make sure of the distance, anticipate where the ball will be, and keep the glove open.

Should the glove start off on the ground as you reach for the ball?

You have to make sure you stay low as you approach the ground ball. You don't want your body to be upright. That goes not only for a second baseman, but for a shortstop or a third baseman, too. By staying low you see the ball better and watch it go into the glove.

How do you throw the ball after making a backhand pickup?

I have to emphasize that when you make a throw, your left shoulder has to be pointed at and facing right toward your **target**. That shoulder does not rise when you make the throw.

Why can't your left shoulder be up high when you make that throw?

Everyone makes mistakes sometimes. Everyone will make a bad throw every now and then. But if your shoulder is up and you make a mistake, you might throw the ball way over the first baseman's head, and no one can catch that. If your shoulder is low and facing the first baseman, you might bounce the ball, and the throw might be a little bit

up the first-base line, but the first baseman still would have a chance to get it.

With a runner at first base, the batter hits a ground ball to your left. How do you get the forceout at second base?

When you catch the ball in the **hole** and turn to second to make the throw, first you have to make sure you're not in line with the runner. You don't want your throw to go in the runner's path and hit the runner.

You have to remember that the most important thing in this situation is to make sure you get the first out, the out at second base. A double play is a bonus. So you have to make sure you throw the ball to the chest of the shortstop, who is covering second base.

How do you make a throw to first base after fielding a ball to your left?

There is a tendency for any player to have the left shoulder **open** when you're throwing to first base from the hole on the right side. Your front shoulder is not facing the first baseman, so you end up making a sidearm throw, which will have a tendency to **tail** away from him. You have to concentrate to make a throw that, even if it does tail, it will go to the first baseman for the out.

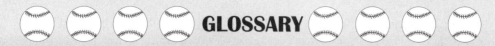 **GLOSSARY**

Backhand: Reaching across with the glove over to the bare-handed side of the body.

Gap: The space between the outfielders, called left-center and right-center, respectively.

Hole: An area between fielders, such as the opening between the second baseman's and the first baseman's positions on the infield.

Hop: A bounce of a ground ball.

Open: Not aimed at the target.

Reading: Watching carefully to get an idea of where the ball is going to bounce, how high it might bounce, and what kind of spin it may have when it gets to the fielder.

Tail: The sideways movement of a ball thrown with a sidearm motion. For a right-handed thrower, the ball will "tail" from left to right as it nears the target.

Target: Where you want to throw the ball.

Easy as 1-2-3!

In general, the second baseman tends to be an overlooked player on any team.

He's usually not a power hitter. He might not be as quick in the field, or have as strong an arm, as the shortstop. But he's steady. That's the term most often applied to a second baseman. He's a player who helps the team win without being the big star. But every now and then, a second baseman will have his moment in the sun, too. Philadelphia Phillies player Mickey Morandini enjoyed his on September 20, 1992.

The Phillies were playing the Pittsburgh Pirates at Pittsburgh's Three Rivers Stadium. The Pirates had Philadelphia pitcher Curt Schilling in a jam in the bottom the sixth inning, with the game tied at 1–1. Andy Van Slyke was on second base and Barry Bonds was on first. Jeff King was the batter.

Schilling threw a pitch, and King hit a line drive that appeared headed up the middle for a base hit. Van Slyke took off from second, hoping to score. Bonds was also on the move.

But Morandini ran a few steps and caught the ball in the air for an out. Then he quickly stepped on the second-base bag, doubling up Van Slyke for the second out on the play. When he saw Bonds coming his way, the alert Morandini ran him down and tagged him out…completing the rare unassisted triple play.

In a matter of seconds, Morandini had gone from being just another very good, steady second baseman to the brightest star on the baseball diamond. But unfortunately for the Phillies, Morandini's brilliance didn't spark them to a win. Pittsburgh ultimately won the game, 3–2.

★ ★

HERE'S THE SITUATION

You're playing second base. Your team is ahead by three runs in the middle innings and there's a runner at first base with one out. The batter hits a soft, high-bouncing ball a little to your left. You take a few steps to your left and you field the ball cleanly.

Should you spin around and throw to second base to get the lead runner out? Or should you just be content with getting the out at first?

HERE'S THE SOLUTION

Make the play to first. It should be a short, simple throw, and you'll probably have plenty of time to get the runner.

Throwing to second could be risky. Yes, you always want to throw out the lead runner whenever you can, but you also want to play smart. You're ahead by three runs, so why take the chance?

If you try to spin around and make the throw to second, the runner could beat the throw. Then the opposition would have two runners on, and only one out. And you'd be in a jam, because the tying run is coming to the plate. So get the easy out. Leave the other team with one runner on at second base, but only one out left in the inning.

Akinori Iwamura's Memories

MY MESSAGE for young players aged eight to twelve is that you have to have fun playing baseball.

In our region, we played more softball at those ages. The game was basically the same, but the big differences from baseball were the size of the ball and the way we threw it.

I lived in Uwajima, in the Ehime Prefecture in Japan. I pitched and played shortstop. I was allowed to throw fastballs and changeups. I remember being in the fourth grade when I threw four games and completed each one in a very hot summer. I was confident at the time. As a batter I was more of a **gap** hitter, but I hit some home runs.

We would practice every day from 3:30 to 7:00 p.m. It was a lot of fun chasing after the ball every day. We used to throw the ball against a wall in the parking lot where I lived, and we even damaged one of the walls of my house!

Back then the spikes we wore cost around $80, and a glove cost about $150.

Sometimes after a game the whole team would go to eat at a Korean BBQ restaurant.

SHORTSTOP

DEREK JETER

The shortstop has to have good range, which is the ability to cover a major part of the infield. He also has to field balls that are hit right at him. Being a successful shortstop begins with good body position, whether charging the ball, fielding it in the **shortstop hole**, or moving to the left for a hard-hit grounder.

In this chapter, All-Star and World Series MVP Derek Jeter offers his suggestions on how to play shortstop.

What's the best body position for fielding a ground ball?

Your legs should be spread apart, maybe shoulder width or a little bit more. You want to make sure your knees are bent. But above all, you have to be comfortable.

Are you standing flat-footed when the ball is coming to you?

No, you want to be on the balls of your feet.

Why on the balls of your feet?

That's the proper stance for any sport. For instance, if you're playing defense in basketball, you have to be on the balls of your feet. Otherwise, you can't move side to side like you need to. If you're flat-footed, someone will make a move and just go right around you. It's the same thing when you're playing baseball. To field ground balls, you have to be able to move from side to side.

What do you do when a ground ball is hit right at you?

First of all, you have to judge how hard the ball is hit. That will tell you if you need to **charge the ball**. Make sure to **read** the hops to see if you should back up a little to field the ball. But, if possible, you want your momentum moving toward first base as you catch the ground ball. That will put you in good position to throw.

What are you looking at when a ground ball is hit to you?

When you're fielding the ball, your eyes are on the ball. You have to watch it all the way into your glove. A lot of times you'll look at the ball and think you have it, but then it might take a **bad hop** at the last second and you won't be able to catch it cleanly. So you have to make sure you watch it all the way.

What do you do with your bare hand when you're catching a ground ball?

You're not going to catch the ball with your bare hand, but it's good to have it next to the glove as support. You want the bare hand as close to the glove as possible, because that way you can get the ball out of the glove a lot quicker to make the throw.

Once you've fielded the ball, how do you throw to first base?

When you're throwing to first, make sure your momentum is going toward the bag. Your body shouldn't go in one direction while you're trying to throw in another. You also want your feet firmly planted underneath you, so your whole body is under control.

It's not necessary to point your left shoulder to where you're throwing, but you should always try to be moving in the same direction as you're throwing.

What do you do on a ground ball to your left?

It depends on how hard it's hit. You have to decide if you can get in front of it, or if you have to play it with one hand. There are a lot of things that come into play when you're making these decisions. Are you playing on grass or turf? How fast is the runner? Was it a right-handed hitter or a left-handed hitter?

What about a ball to your right?

That's probably the hardest play, if you have to catch the ball on your **backhand**. In that situation, you're running away from first base when you field the ball. So when you do get the ball, you have to quickly redirect your momentum to first to make the throw. That's the toughest thing to do. And it's also the longest throw.

You have to gather yourself and get your body under control, if you can. Sometimes you might have to throw off-balance, though. It all depends on how much time you have.

How do you make a backhand pickup?

Ideally, you'd like to get the ball going to the middle of your left foot. That way, you don't have to really reach for the ball. But sometimes, if the ball is hit hard, you don't have a choice and you have to get it any way you can.

How do you make a throw from the *shortstop hole?*

You have to make sure you **plant** yourself. Get the ball, stop, gather yourself, and then throw. You put your right foot down, push off that foot, and throw.

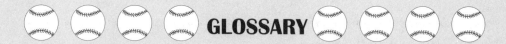 **GLOSSARY**

Backhand: Reaching across with the glove over to the bare-handed side of the body.

Bad hop: A ball that doesn't bounce in a predictable manner. It may bounce unexpectedly to the left or right or even up high.

Charging a ball: Moving forward toward the ball rather than staying in your position and waiting for the ball to come to you.

Planting: Pressing a foot into the ground.

Reading: Watching carefully to get an idea of where the ball is going to bounce, how high it might bounce, and what kind of spin it may have when it gets to the fielder.

Shortstop hole: The space on the infield dirt between the third baseman and the shortstop.

A Pebble Rocks the Yankees!

The moment when the ball left Bill Virdon's bat, it appeared as if the Pittsburgh Pirates outfielder had hit into a double play that would leave the New York Yankees only four outs shy of another World Championship.

But there was no double play. The ball hit a pebble in the dirt at shortstop, which caused it to take an unexpected hop up, striking Yankees' shortstop, Tony Kubek, in the throat.

Kubek fell to the ground in pain as the ball bounced away. Virdon was safe at first, and the lead runner was safe at second on the bad-hop single. So instead of having two outs and no one on base, the Pirates now had two men on and no outs. And they took advantage of the big break by scoring five runs in the inning for a 9–7 lead.

The Yankees rallied to tie the game at 9–9 in the top of the ninth inning, but all that did was set up second baseman Bill Mazeroski to become the toast of Pittsburgh and the baseball world. Mazeroski slugged a home run in the bottom of the ninth, giving the Pirates a 10–9 win and the 1960 World Championship. But while it was Mazeroski's home run that eventually won Pittsburgh the World Series title, it was a tiny pebble that really helped the Pirates rock the Yankees.

★★★★★★★★★★★★★★★★★★★★★★★★★★★★★★★★★★

HERE'S THE SITUATION

There's a runner at third base, with one out, in the last inning. You're playing shortstop, and your team is ahead by four runs. You're playing back at
your normal position. The batter hits a hard ground ball to you. The runner
from third breaks for home. You know he doesn't have great speed, and the
ball is hit pretty hard to you. You field the ball cleanly.

Where should you throw?

Home?

Or first?

HERE'S THE SOLUTION

Get the easier out: throw to first base.

You might be able to throw the runner out at home, but it's a tougher
play because it's not a forceout. The catcher will have to grab the ball and
apply a tag before the runner hits home plate. There's too much risk in this
type of play—the ball could be knocked out of the glove by a sliding runner,
the catcher could miss the ball, or your throw might be off-line.

It's not worth the risk. If the runner does score, you're still up three runs,
and once you get the runner out at first base, you'll have two outs in the last
inning.

★★ Derek Jeter's Memories ★★

I JUST REMEMBER the whole Little League thing...being out there trying to act like everyone I'd see on TV, pretending I was a big league player. I was a Yankee fan, so I pretended to be all of the Yankees at some point.

We moved around a lot when I was a kid. I played in the Westwood Little League, the Oakwood league, and the Eastwood league. They were all in Michigan.

You always have to have a good time. If you have fun and practice every chance you get, you're going to be successful.

THIRD BASE

EVAN LONGORIA

There are times when a third baseman doesn't need a glove to make a play. He can just use his bare hand. But fielding a slow roller or a bunt that way can be tough, especially if you're on the run.

In this chapter, American League Rookie of the Year and All-Star Evan Longoria talks about how to make this difficult play, as well as tips on other aspects of playing third base.

While you're in your *stance* as a third baseman, what do you look at to see if a batter might be bunting for a base hit?

Sometimes the batter may be holding the bat at a different angle, or maybe the batter does something different with the bat. Maybe if a hitter usually has a **wiggle in the bat** as he gets ready for the pitch, he might stop the wiggle before getting ready to bunt. Hitters planning to bunt may change their hand position on the bat or keep their bodies still.

Or sometimes even the batter's facial expression will give it away. Sometimes you see him take a peek toward third base to see where the third baseman is playing.

Get in the habit of observing batters carefully. There are a lot of different little signs that can tell you a batter is going to bunt.

So you, as a third baseman, are concentrating on the batter?

I'm always looking at the batter whether he's a bunter or not. But certain guys are more likely to bunt. For example, the number four hitter is not going to bunt. But obviously when number one or number nine is in the box, I'm looking for signs that he's planning to bunt.

And when a ball is bunted, or if there is a slow roller hit toward third base, how do you approach making that play?

There are different ways. If it's a slow roller and a slow runner is running, you want to attack the ball aggressively. You try to get around the ball, field it with your glove, and be moving toward first base as you field it.

What do you mean by "getting around it?"

As you run in, you have to make a semicircle toward the foul line and then back toward first base when you field the ball. This way you can get your momentum going toward first base when you make your throw.

How do you make a bare-handed play?

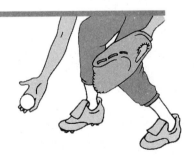

As you're bending down to pick up the ball, if you're a right-handed thrower, you want to be stepping forward with your left foot. Then get your feet in the correct position so you can make a good throw to first base after you have picked up the ball. But the biggest thing is making sure you've picked up the ball. You can't make the play without getting the ball off the ground!

Do you pick up the ball from the top or scoop it up?

You want to stay underneath the ball with your bare hand and try and scoop it from the ground up. You want to get your fingers underneath the ball.

How do you make the throw after making the bare-handed pickup?

You usually throw with a **sidearm** or **underhand** motion. Be careful, because you're going to have to judge quickly where you're going to aim the throw. When you throw with this type of motion and **arm angle**, the ball is going to **tail** back toward the first-base line. So you have to aim a little more to the second-base position because the throw will tail back toward the first baseman.

How hard do you charge in to make this play?

You have to get there with some speed, but at the same time you have to be under control. If you're rushing and out of control, the chances are you're not going to be able to pick up the ball while you're running at full speed. So you want to run as fast as you can to about five feet from the ball and then start **breaking down** to scoop it up.

When you make this play, you have to be low enough to the ground to be able to get the ball off the ground. The biggest issues are being under control yourself and knowing who is running and how fast that person is.

Why is it important to know the speed of the batter who is running to first base?

If you have a fast guy running, you probably need to go 40 percent faster and try and throw the ball quicker than if you have a slow runner moving. With a slower runner, you can take a little more time and make sure you're under control.

How do the mechanics of the bare-handed pickup and throw on a slow roller or a bunt compare to a routine ground ball to third?

On a routine ground ball, the ball gets to you faster, but for the most part, you know how much time you have to throw to first base, and you're able to process that information in your usual way. The scoop of the ball and the throw to first base has to happen much quicker. But with the slow roller or bunt you have a lot more variables going around in your mind at once. Handling the ball in these situations calls for more complicated mechanics and can take more time.

What are the mechanics of fielding and throwing to first base on a routine ground ball?

After fielding the ball, you have to get your body into whatever position you're comfortable throwing in. Everything depends on how good your arm is. If you don't have a strong arm, you have to really get your body and momentum going toward first. But a guy who has a tremendous arm can probably just stand straight up and make a strong throw to first.

For me, the primary objective is to catch the ball. Then you reset your feet. I try to point my left shoulder to first base to make a good, accurate throw. Usually you make an **overhand** throw on a routine play.

Is playing third base the same as playing shortstop?

You can't play third base like it's the shortstop position. Third base is more of a reaction position. I think playing shortstop is more like being in a dance out there on the field. You have to have rhythm and you have to be ready to go in either direction.

At third base, you can be down in your fielding stance a lot earlier and be ready right away to move from that stance, because you have to be able to dive and take one hard step to your right or left and field the ball. There are not really a lot of plays where you're going to take four or five steps and field a ground ball the way you do at shortstop.

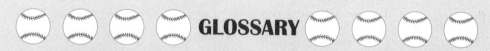

GLOSSARY

Arm angle: The position of your arm as you throw the ball.

Breaking down: Slowing down.

Over the top/overhand: A throwing motion in which the arm comes up close to and past the ear when releasing the ball.

Sidearm: A throwing motion in which the arm is about waist-high and parallel to the ground upon release of the ball.

Stance: A player's body position.

Stirrups: Worn over socks, stirrups have just a strap of fabric that loops under the middle of the foot. Usually of a contrasting color to the socks.

Tail: The sideways movement of a ball thrown with a sidearm motion. For a right-handed thrower, the ball will "tail" from left to right as it nears the target.

Underhand: A throwing motion in which the palm of the hand faces up toward the sky. Generally a soft, but firm, toss.

Wiggle in the bat: Movement of the bat back and forth as a hitter awaits a pitch.

Triple the Fun, Twice!

Triple plays don't happen very often. But on July 17, 1990, at Fenway Park, the Boston Red Sox grounded into a triple play. Not once...but twice in the same game! And both times, it was Minnesota's Gary Gaetti, Al Newman, and Kent Hrbek who tripled the Twins' fun and snuffed out any possible Red Sox rallies.

In the fourth inning, the bases were loaded. The Red Sox had put Minnesota pitcher Scott Erickson in deep trouble. But on Erickson's next pitch, Tom Brunansky hit a hard grounder to Gaetti, the Twins' third baseman. Gaetti caught the ball, right near the third-base bag. He calmly stepped on the base. One out. Then he threw to Newman, covering second base, and Newman stepped on that bag. Two outs. Newman quickly relayed the ball to Hrbek, Minnesota's first baseman. The throw beat Brunansky. Three outs...a triple play! There were high fives all around as the Twins raced to their dugout.

In the eighth inning, there was a virtual instant replay. This time, there were runners on first and second base, and up stepped Red Sox batter Jody Reed to the plate. Reed hit the ball on the ground, right at Gaetti. The third baseman stepped on the bag and threw to Newman at second. Newman relayed the ball to Hrbek. Once again, the Twins had pulled off a triple play!

It was the first time in Major League history that one team had turned two triple plays in the same game. The Red Sox, however, had the last laugh. Boston won the game, 1–0.

★ ★

HERE'S THE SITUATION

It's the last inning. You're up by one run. There's one out and the opposing team has runners at first and third. You're playing third base and the batter hits a hard one-hopper right at you. The runner from third breaks for home as soon as the ball is hit.

Do you throw home in an attempt to cut down the tying run at the plate? Or should you try for a double play, which could end the game and give your team the victory?

HERE'S THE SOLUTION

There's really no easy answer here. You need to figure out what to do as the ball is approaching you. A lot of information must be processed quickly.

Is the ball hit straight at you?

How fast a runner is the batter?

If the answers to those questions are "Yes, the ball is coming right to me," and "No, the batter doesn't run well," then you may want to take a chance on turning the game-ending double play.

But if the ball isn't hit to you that hard or if the batter is pretty fast, your odds of turning the double play are slim. In this case, you might want to throw home to stop the tying run from scoring.

No matter what, you want to make sure you get at least one out on the play, whether it's at home, second, or even at first base.

Evan Longoria's Memories

I GREW UP in Downey, California. I played baseball starting at age four, from T-ball all the way up.

My dad was my coach from the time I was very young until the time I was in eighth grade, when I told him I wanted to move on and play for another coach. He was never really that hard on me, but I didn't want the other kids to think I was being favored because my dad was the coach.

For the most part I played shortstop and I pitched. Was I a good pitcher? No. I was a good athlete, but I never really threw hard. I did some pitching in high school out of necessity.

I played in a league called the Savio Patriots. It was a Catholic School, St. Dominic's Savio, and they had a baseball league. They had four teams, so I played that until I was seven or eight, and then I moved over to the DJAA [Downey Junior Athletic Association]. I played in the Downey Little League. That's where I met a lot of kids who are still my best friends today.

There were four good, advanced twelve- and thirteen-year-olds when I played in that league—kids who were full-grown at that age, kids like you see at the Little League World Series throwing 70 miles an hour. I remember facing them a handful of times, and I dreaded it because they were really throwing gas in there. It wasn't a fun day when we faced them.

I was a line-drive hitter. I hit some home runs, but I wasn't really a home-run hitter until I got to college. I wasn't physically mature. I wasn't fast, either. I could just hit. I hit for average.

I was always excited to go play. The first team I played with wore stirrups and I would end up crying when I put my **stirrups** on because the hook of material underneath my foot was so uncomfortable. I really hated putting those on. Finally they got me the two-in-one socks, and I was a lot happier. They were red and white.

After some games we would go to a pizza joint where they had video games. We would go there and hang out. We had a lot of the team parties there. It was a fun time.

THE DOUBLE PLAY

JIMMY ROLLINS

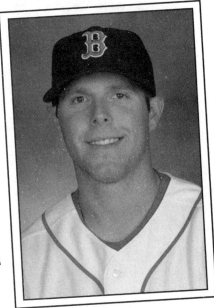

DUSTIN PEDROIA

I t's called "The Pitcher's Best Friend." Or "The Twin Killing." But no matter what its nickname, there's nothing that helps a pitcher get out of a jam faster than the double play. It requires quick, efficient teamwork performed with ballet-like precision, resulting in two outs on one ground ball.

In this chapter, National League MVP and All-Star short-stop Jimmy Rollins and American League MVP, Rookie of the Year, and All-Star second baseman Dustin Pedroia talk about how to "turn two." They discuss the responsibilities of each position and the techniques they use in turning the 6-4-3 and 4-6-3 double plays.

THE 6-4-3 DOUBLE PLAY
[SHORTSTOP TO SECOND BASEMAN TO FIRST BASEMAN]

JIMMY ROLLINS
THE SHORTSTOP'S RESPONSIBILITIES

Do you position yourself any differently in a double-play situation?

Well, in general you try to cut in half the distance to second base from your normal positioning. I usually play on the dirt right in front of the outfield grass, so from there, in a double-play situation, I probably take four or five steps in.

Why do you want to cut down that distance?

You need to make two throws to get that hitter out at first base.

When you're in a normal position, without a double-play possibility, you can take your time because you need only one strong throw to get the hitter out at first after fielding a ground ball. In a double-play situation there's going to be a stop, a change of direction (a throw to second base), and then another throw (from the second baseman to first).

In a double play, sometimes you're going to feed the ball to him **overhand** and sometimes you're going to feed it to him **underhand**, and that's why you have to shorten the distance so the ball gets to you quicker at shortstop. When you are closer, you can then get the ball to the second baseman quicker, so he can get rid of the ball and have enough time to get out of the way of the runner and still get the out at first.

Is there a best body position to use when catching the ball if you're going to start a double play?

You just catch the ball as if you're fielding a regular grounder and getting ready to throw to first. But when you're starting a double play, from then on your body position is different. When you get the ball, you don't pull your body all the way up to make the throw, like you do if you're throwing to first base.

Your body comes up from the ground from fielding the ball only high enough to give you a good arm position to throw to the second baseman.

Where do you have your glove when you're getting ready to field the ball? On the ground?

That's just a matter of comfort. Fielding is just like hitting, everybody starts differently. You just have to get to the ball correctly, in a good position to field it. When you get to the ball, you want to have the palm of the glove facing up, and you better catch it because you can't start a double play until you catch the ball.

What's the most important part of giving the second baseman a feed to turn a double play?

You have to make sure he sees the ball when you're giving it to him.

On balls to your right, going away from you, you'll be farther away from the second baseman and he will have a chance to **pick up** the ball. But when you field a ball hit closer to the bag, it will be harder for him to pick up the ball. Obviously in this situation it's more important for you to make sure he can see the ball right away because that's going to determine his timing.

Everything you do in trying to turn a double play is done to save time. One-tenth of a second can be the difference between the runner being safe or out at first base.

How do you make the throw after you field a ground ball to your right?

If you're going to your right, toward your backhand side [for a right-handed player], you want your arm in a position to give your second baseman a good feed. After fielding the ball, you don't want to come up too high to make a totally overhand throw because that wastes time, so you throw with more of a **sidearm** motion.

Making a sidearm throw depends on your comfort level. I basically take my arm up and flip the throw from my hip. I know how to throw the ball from that angle so the second baseman is going to get it in a good spot. That kind of confidence comes from playing the game and learning your skills and practicing that throw; but in general, you want to make a nice level throw to the second baseman.

What if it's a ground ball to your left, more *up the middle* and close to the bag? What type of throw do you make in that situation?

If the ball gets to you closer to the base, you want to make what's called a little shovel-pass type of throw to the second baseman. In that instance you don't come up with your body much at all after fielding the ball. It can be an underhand toss or a backhand flip, depending on where the ball has taken you.

The most routine throw is the underhand toss to the second baseman. You take the ball out of your glove with your bare hand, pull your glove back a little, and move your bare hand forward so the second baseman can see the ball immediately. That way he can judge his timing and won't be surprised about where the ball is coming from. Even though the toss is soft and it's easier to turn a double play on a grounder that's close to the bag, things get quicker, too, because there's less distance covered during that toss.

Where do you want to throw the ball to the second baseman?

A good feed can be anywhere from the waist to about the shoulders. You don't want to get that feed up around the second baseman's eyes because if the ball is up there, when he goes to catch the ball, his glove could block his vision and he might miss it. But if you throw it between the waist and shoulders, on either side, he should be able to handle it easily.

DUSTIN PEDROIA
The Second Baseman's Responsibilities

How do you position yourself to turn this double play?

The direction of the throw dictates what you need to do to position yourself to turn the double play.

What is the normal positioning in the field for a second baseman in a double-play situation?

I'll scoot in two steps probably and then one step toward second base to make sure I can get there on time. But I don't want to come in too far and give up too much range in case the batter hits a ball to the right or left of me. I just want to make sure I'm in position to be flexible and field any ball that's hit to me.

If the ground ball is hit to shortstop, what do you do?

I get to the back part of second base as fast as I can.

I like to get there early to make sure my feet are underneath me, to make sure I'm balanced. That way, if it's a bad feed I'm always ready for it, and if the feed is right where I want it, it's a nice routine play.

If you get to the base late and there's a bad throw, you won't have time to react to it, and you might even miss the ball.

What are the most important elements for a second base-man in turning this double play?

Getting to the bag early is the biggest thing. Catching the ball is second. You have to make sure you catch the ball and then, of course, you try to throw accurately to first base. You have to practice this play a lot, so when it comes up in a game, you can just get the ball out of your glove and throw it.

What is the position of your feet at the base?

I like to be at the back part of the base, the side that's facing the center fielder. That helps protect you from the runner sliding into you.

My left foot is on the outside edge of the base. Then wherever the feed is will dictate where I go from there.

What do you do with your feet as the ball is coming to you?

I move my feet so I can try to get my front [left] foot down and **planted** on the ground, and as I do that I get my shoulders turned toward first base, with my left shoulder pointed at the first baseman.

Why do you want to be in that body position?

That way you'll have a better chance to make an accurate throw. If your shoulder isn't turned to first base and your foot isn't down, your arm is going to **fly open** and you're going to throw the ball up the first-base line because it won't go straight, it will **tail** on you.

Getting your foot down helps you square up your shoulders to second base.

What does "squared up to the base" mean when you're making the pivot?

It means your left shoulder is lined up and pointing at first base.

If you turn so the left shoulder is past first base, your upper body will rotate, your elbow will drop down, and your throw will tail up the first-base line and the first baseman will have to step off the base to make the catch. Or if you exaggerate the turn to get the throw to first from that body position, you might yank the ball to the right-field side of first base.

So you want to have your shoulders straight in line with first base. If you do that, you're going to make a solid throw.

Where do you want your hands to be when making the pivot?

You try to keep them as close to your right ear as possible as you receive the ball so you can get the ball out of the glove and quickly get into your throwing motion.

Don't reach out to catch the ball. Keep your hands close into your body. That way you can get rid of the ball faster and you are always in position to throw it at any angle. If you need to throw it sidearm or **stay on top**, you'll be in position to do it.

How about your bare hand?

You want it close to the glove. Both hands are right there together as you catch the ball because you want to be able to make a quick transfer of the ball from the glove to the throwing hand. You want to be quick and you want a good grip on the ball.

Do you always stay at the bag? Do you come across the bag?

If the throw is right to me, I stay at the bag and use arm strength to get the ball to the first baseman, and I'm able to use the bag as protection from the sliding runner. But if the throw is a little bit to the left of me then I will come across the bag and throw that way.

How do you set your feet as you come across the bag?

My biggest thing is to touch the base with my right foot and have my momentum carry me across, and then throw as I cross the bag. If you use this method, you have to be athletic enough to be able to throw on the run. If you're not able to do that, then you need to stop, set your feet, and make a good throw.

How do you grip the ball when you're making your throw?

However it gets to you. Sometimes you don't have time to adjust the ball to a specific type of grip. You just get the ball and throw it.

What's more important in turning the double play—quick hands or quick feet?

Obviously if you have both you're going to turn a really good double play. But if you have one or the other, you need to stay with your strength.

If you have a strong arm and good hands, you need to stay at the back part of the base. Just catch it and throw it. But if you have good feet and don't have a strong arm, then you need to move your feet to get yourself into position to get rid of the ball as fast as possible.

THE 4-6-3 DOUBLE PLAY
[Second baseman to Shortstop to First Baseman]

DUSTIN PEDROIA
The Second Baseman's Responsibilities

What's the most important aspect of this play from a second baseman's point of view?

My biggest priority is to get the ball to the shortstop early and let him do his job.

It doesn't matter if the ball is coming right at you, you can move your feet and give him an underhand flip throw, or you can stay there and go to one knee and throw it, or side-shuffle your feet and throw it to him.

There are a ton of different ways to turn the double play, but the most important thing is to catch the ball and get it to the shortstop as fast as possible. It doesn't matter how you do it.

I used to play shortstop and my thinking was that if I had the ball early, there was a good chance we were going to turn it.

What is the best-scenario body position to field the ball to start a double play?

If it's a routine double play, I open up a bit by putting my right foot a little farther back than my left foot to allow myself to get rid of the ball more quickly.

But sometimes it might be a hard-hit ball and you have to stay in front of it in case it takes a **bad hop**, so you can't open up the same way. In that situation you have to square yourself up to the ball, field it, and then make a good throw. The biggest thing on plays like that is to catch the ball first.

When do you make an underhand flip? When do you make a more overhand type of throw?

On any ground ball hit to the right of the second baseman I think you should flip the ball underhand to the shortstop. It's a higher percentage play than throwing the ball overhand. This way the shortstop will see the ball better if it's underhand, with your hand open, the palm up, and the ball exposed.

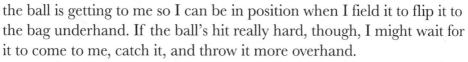

If the ball is hit right at me, I have good feet, so I will try to move my feet as the ball is getting to me so I can be in position when I field it to flip it to the bag underhand. If the ball's hit really hard, though, I might wait for it to come to me, catch it, and throw it more overhand.

There are a lot of ways to turn it, but as long as you catch the ball and get it to shortstop quickly it's the right play.

What do you do on a ball that's hit two or three steps to the second baseman's left?

Same thing. I try to get to the ball quickly enough so I can open up my right foot as I field it. My right foot isn't parallel to my left foot, but a little back. I make sure I field the ball first and then throw the ball **three-quarters** with a **four-seam** spin on the ball so the shortstop can then get rid of it as fast as he can.

Where do you want to throw the ball?

I try to throw the ball to the back edge of the base all the time because that's where the shortstop is coming across.

How high do you want the throw to the shortstop?

Anywhere from the belt to the face is a good feed. The shortstop can do a lot of things with a throw around there. If it's lower than that he might have a tough time turning it.

JIMMY ROLLINS
THE SHORTSTOP'S RESPONSIBILITIES

In a double-play situation, when the ball is hit to the second baseman, what does the shortstop do?

The first thing you do is go to the bag. Not necessarily as fast as you can, but at a good pace. Everything is timing. It's hard to explain, but fielding is like dancing. Being an infielder, you have to have footwork. We say you have to know how to dance around the bag because it's timing and footwork, same as in dancing.

I try to get to a step behind the bag—on the back side of the bag, the side closest to the outfield—as the second baseman is actually getting the ball in his possession.

What do you do when the second baseman is throwing you the ball?

When he gets ready to throw the ball, I take my right foot and put it on the back corner of the bag expecting the throw and expecting to go toward the ball. I use the bag basically as a starting block to push off and give myself distance across the bag to get out of the runner's way.

110

Why do you put your foot on the corner of the bag and not right on top of it?

You don't want to be in the middle of the bag because if you are, when you press off the bag, your foot might slip and then you might get hurt when the runner slides in. You want to find a corner of the bag to push off from and clear yourself from the runner.

Why else do you want to push off the bag instead of staying there and making the throw from the bag?

It gives you a clear throwing lane to the first baseman if you push off. The runner won't be in your way.

Also, by doing this, you're going to meet the ball on the throw from the second baseman, shortening the distance the ball is traveling. The quicker you get the ball, the quicker you can make the throw to first. As the throw comes from the second baseman, you're reading that throw, seeing where it is going and where you have to move to go out and get it.

Where are your hands when you receive the ball? Is your bare hand right next to your glove?

Not really. When you go after the ball with two hands, a lot of times you're going to limit your range. If you get used to having the two hands together, when you have to extend to get the ball, that's more difficult to do.

You can't expect the perfect throw. Your second baseman might be perfect most of the time, but that one time he's a little off you might **get handcuffed** or not come up cleanly with the ball. Now it looks like he made a bad throw when you could have been—and should have been—ready to go get that ball.

So it doesn't matter where your bare hand is?

You want it close enough so you can make the transfer, but keep in mind you still have to get your bare hand up to your throwing side anyway, no matter where you catch the ball.

What kind of throw do you make to first?

Basically, your body doesn't necessarily have to be in a typical throwing position when you turn a double play. Sometimes your shoulders aren't squared up to first base as they might be on a routine play from shortstop. You don't always have that opportunity.

So how do make an accurate throw to first if you can't be squared up?

To me, personally, I like to get the ball from the second baseman and get my throwing arm on a good straight line to the first baseman. I could be running away from the bag, with my body maybe taking me toward right field, but as long as my arm is lined up, my release point will be on line with the first baseman.

If you're on the move like this and your throwing arm is not in line with the first baseman, there's more of a chance you might make a throw that is wild, up the first-base line and into the runner, making it harder for the first baseman to stretch for the ball.

As you get older, your arm gets stronger and you understand that you can't always square yourself up, so you have to find a way, even if you are fading away with your body, to keep your throwing side and arm on line. That way even if you don't make a perfect throw, it will be easier for him to make a stretch for it.

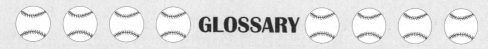 **GLOSSARY**

Bad hop: A ball that doesn't bounce in a predictable manner. It may bounce unexpectedly to the left or right or even up high.

Fly open: A throwing position in which the front shoulder is turned too far away from the target, exposing the chest.

Four-seam grip: A grip of the baseball in which the fingers are positioned across, not with, the four seams of the ball. This grip produces a rotation that keeps the ball moving in a straight line.

Getting handcuffed: Trying to field a ball with the hands too close to the body. Often, the ball will hit off the heel of the glove and not make it into the web or pocket, making the catch more difficult.

Over the top/Overhand: A throwing motion in which the arm comes up close to and past the ear when releasing the ball.

Picking up: Looking for and finding a particular target.

Planting: Pressing a foot into the ground.

Sidearm: A throwing motion in which the arm is about waist-high and parallel to the ground upon release of the ball.

Staying on top: Throwing in an overhand motion.

Tail: The sideways movement of a ball thrown with a sidearm motion. For a right-handed thrower, the ball will "tail" from left to right as it nears the target.

Three-quarters: A throwing motion in which the arm is halfway between the position for an overhand throw and a sidearm throw.

Underhand: A throwing motion in which the palm of the hand faces up toward the sky. Generally a soft, but firm, toss.

Up the middle: The area in the middle of the baseball diamond—through the pitcher's mound, past second base, and into center field.

Yer Out!

Boston Red Sox runner Dwight Evans was perched at third base, and Rich Gedman was at first base, after grounding a single to right field. There was one out in the top of the fifth inning, and the Sox were trailing the Oakland Athletics, 6–5, in Game 3 of the 1988 American League Championship Series. Oakland already had a 2–0 lead in the best-of-seven series, so the Red Sox were getting desperate, trying to scratch for every run they could.

Gene Nelson was pitching for Oakland. The next Red Sox batter was Jody Reed, who hit a bouncer to the third baseman, Carney Lansford. His throw to second was in plenty of time to get Gedman for the second out of the inning.

Gedman slid hard into the second baseman, Mike Gallego, so Reed was safe at first. Evans scored what appeared to be the tying run. But the second base umpire Ken Kaiser ruled that Gedman had gone out of the baseline in his slide, which is a violation of the rules. As a result, Reed was also called out on the play. The Red Sox vehemently protested the umpire's call, but to no avail.

Gedman and Reed were called out on the double play, so Evans's run didn't count. The Athletics maintained their 6–5 lead. And Boston never caught up. The Red Sox lost the game, 10–6. They lost the next day, too, as Oakland swept the series and earned a berth in the World Series.

HERE'S THE SITUATION

It's the bottom of the last inning. There are runners at first and third with only one out, and you have a 4–3 lead. A ground ball is hit to you at shortstop.

Should you try to turn a double play, even though the tying run will score if you fail? Or should you field the ball, check the runner at third to see what he's doing, and then make your decision?

HERE'S THE SOLUTION

What should you do? Well, it depends.

There are a lot of little facts you need to know in making this decision. How fast is the runner? How hard was the ball hit? Where was the ball hit? Is it an easy double-play ball? How good is the second baseman at turning a double play?

Whatever you do, you have to make a decision fast. In this situation, there isn't one correct answer. All you can do is try to make the best decision, and do so as quickly as possible!

Dustin Pedroia's Memories

I REMEMBER playing Little League in Woodland, California. It was fun. There was good competition and everyone wanted to win.

I was on the Indians when I was in the Majors. We only lost one game in three years, so that was fun. I kind of lucked out playing shortstop and pitching. I was a pretty good pitcher. I just threw a fastball and a curveball. I put my uniform on at two o'clock in the afternoon to get ready for a seven o'clock game. It was a blast.

After games parents would switch off getting snacks for the kids, maybe a Rice Krispie treat or a juice box.

I was one of the smallest kids out there. I wasn't that small, but there were definitely some kids bigger than me. I hit home runs and I threw hard. I hit a lot of bombs.

Jimmy Rollins's Memories

I JUST REMEMBER a whole bunch of winning.

I first started playing organized ball when I was eight. I wasn't a shortstop all the time. I rotated mostly between short and third. There was a guy who later played in the Detroit Tigers' organization who played shortstop before me, and I looked up to him. He was older and he was good. I wanted to be like Cal Ripken or Ozzie Smith.

We didn't have fences in our field, but I did hit balls that got by a lot of guys and I ran and touched all four. So did I have power? I don't know, but I hit the gaps.

I grew up playing in Oakland, California, about a mile from the Oakland Coliseum. It was called Greenman Field. It was all dirt. We had stands. The field for eleven- to twelve-year-olds was the pride and joy. It had fences, a scoreboard, a grandstand, everything.

All the other fields were spread around, one facing this way, another facing another way. Every once in a while you'd get the fourteen- and fifteen-year-olds playing at the same time, and you'd have a ball come from their game flying through our field. You'd have to call time out and go get it. It was an automatic triple if time needed to be called, but if it could be played cleanly you could keep on running.

When I first started playing for A&T Travel, our uniforms

were black and gold, Pittsburgh Pirates colors. Then I played with Allen Temple, which was a church. Those uniforms were white and gold. On all-stars, though, our uniforms were green and white when I was eight to eleven, and when I turned twelve they were blue and white.

I pitched all the way through high school. I wasn't sneaky fast—no sneak behind it—just straight fast. But shortstop was my best position. I didn't want to be a pitcher. Pitching was fun, but I liked shortstop—you could dive, turn a double play. That was the glory to me.

I'm one of the smaller guys in the big leagues, but back then I was right along with everybody else. They all kept growing. I don't know what happened to me.

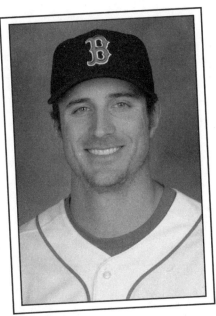

CATCHING FLY BALLS

ROCCO BALDELLI

OUTFIELD

Standing all the way in the outfield, it may seem like you're far away from the action. Many innings can go by without you being involved in a play. But you can't let your mind wander. You have to be ready for action at all times. When a ball is hit in the air toward you, you have to track it down.

In this chapter, Rocco Baldelli discusses a few basics of outfield play.

What's going through your mind as you stand in the outfield?

Well, no matter what outfield position I'm in, I'm basically looking at the pitcher's release of the ball and the path of the ball going into the plate. And then I'm trying to read the swing off the bat, whether the guy's going to be a bit early or late on it.

Why is it important to *read* the swing?

The swing tells you at what angle the ball's going to come off the bat, and it helps you get a good **jump** and anticipate where the ball is going.

Normally you can kind of lean one way or the other, especially if you're playing center field. For instance, if you see that the pitch is away from the hitter as it approaches the plate, and if you understand that that guy hits the ball the other way a lot, you know the ball is probably going to go to the **opposite field**. So you can be leaning toward the opposite field, ready to run in that direction, anticipating that the ball will be hit there.

How do you stand in the outfield? What's your "ready" position?

I usually just have my legs spread a little bit wider than my shoulders and I stand on the balls of my feet, maybe leaning forward a bit.

Why on the balls of your feet?

I think it helps you move. When the ball is hit, you've got to go right away. If you are on your heels, you're not really going to be ready to run and make a play.

What about your hands?

Usually they're just hanging down, a little bit away from my thighs.

Why do you watch the ball out of the pitcher's hand? Why don't you just concentrate on the spot where the ball hits the bat?

I think if you just watch the bat, your timing may be off a little bit and you may not be ready to go after the ball if it's hit your way. If you're just standing and looking at the batter I don't think you'll get a good jump on the ball. It's kind of a rhythm thing. You watch the ball from the pitcher, you get on the balls of your feet, and you get ready to go after the ball.

There are times when there's not a lot of action in the outfield. How do you keep your mind from wandering?

You learn to stay in the game mentally. You have to know what's going on in the game, what the situation is, because that is going to affect what you do as an outfielder if the ball comes to you. Paying attention helps you make quick decisions. If you stay mentally in the game you're going to be ready to make any play possible.

Yeah, there are times when you may not get very much action out there, but you have to do your best to be ready every pitch because you never know when that action might be coming, and it might be coming at a crucial time.

When the ball goes in the air, and it's a nice lazy fly ball and an easy catch, how do you want to haul in the ball?

A lot of that comes naturally to every player.

I don't know if there's a right way to make a catch or not as long as you figure out a way that you're comfortable with and that works for you. Normally you want to catch the ball on your throwing-hand side with your glove up around your head, but try not to block your view of the ball with your glove as you move it to make the catch. With practice over time you learn how to do that.

If there's no one on base, the object is just to catch the ball. If there are people on base and you have to get the ball back to the infield in a hurry, you would probably position yourself a couple of steps behind where the ball is coming down so you have some momentum as you move in for the catch. That way you can make a strong throw after catching the ball.

How do the sun and wind affect an outfielder? What can you do to minimize their effect?

The sun and the wind affect you all the time in the outfield. That's one thing a lot of people don't notice when they're watching a game, but outfielders are continually fighting the sun and the wind. Sometimes that makes it really difficult to catch a fly ball.

When it's really sunny out, it helps to wear sunglasses, but often you end up having to shield the sun with your glove or with your throwing hand so you can try to see the ball. Sometimes at night you have to shield your eyes the same way if a ball goes in front of the lights.

At what point do you try to shield the sun?

You know the sun could be a problem for any clear, daytime game. You have to check the sun's position before the first pitch of every inning. You have to be prepared for the sun being a problem.

When the ball is anywhere around the sun, I put my glove up in the air, directly in line with the sun, and I try to keep my eye on the ball, peeking around the glove. Sometimes you have to play the ball a little bit to your side instead of getting right under it if that's the best way you can see the ball.

How do you check out the wind?

Well, in the big leagues there are flags at the field, so you check out the flags to see which way they're blowing. In batting practice when you're in the outfield you pay attention to what the ball is doing in the wind that day. You can do that in any league, even if there aren't flags around. But when batters are big and they hit the ball high, the wind can affect what the ball does and the outfielders have to be ready to react accordingly. You can also pick up a blade of grass and toss it into the air to see which way the wind might be blowing.

Do you want to catch a fly ball with one hand or two?

In the outfield I don't think that matters, but I don't think it could hurt to catch the ball with two hands.

Every kid is taught to always catch the ball with two hands, with the bare hand next to the glove as the ball settles into the glove just in case the ball starts to fall out. But that's not always practical when you're out there, and it doesn't always work the best when you're trying to make a play. Where the ball comes down can dictate how you catch it. You may have to reach for it, and then it's tough to catch it with two hands.

I think because a lot of players catch with two hands as young kids they get comfortable doing it and they continue doing it in the big leagues. So I would say if you're more comfortable catching the ball with two hands, then do that.

 GLOSSARY

Jump: A quick start toward a target.

Opposite field: For a right-handed hitter, the opposite field is right field; for a left-handed hitter, the opposite field is left field.

Reading: Another way of saying "judging the ball." Understanding where the ball may come down.

That's Using His Head!

On May 26, 1993, Jose Canseco gave Cleveland's Carlos Martinez a home run by using his head. Literally.

In the fourth inning of the game, Martinez hit a long fly ball that sailed toward the fence in right-center field. Canseco, playing right field for the Texas Rangers, drifted back on the ball. His body was angled with his right shoulder closest to the wall. As he reached the warning track, Canseco reached up with his glove hand. But the ball didn't go in his glove. In fact, it didn't even touch his glove. Canseco had missed the ball—completely. The ball hit the top of Canseco's head—and plopped over the fence for a home run!

★★★★★★★★★★★★★★★★★★★★★★★★★★★★★★★★★

HERE'S THE SITUATION

There are runners at first and second. It's the last inning. There is one out and your team is ahead by two runs. You're playing right field. The batter hits a fly ball toward right-center. You take off after the ball, but quickly realize it will not be an easy, routine catch. To have any chance of catching the ball, you're going to have to dive for it.

Should you dive for it? Or should you play it safe and just give the batter a single?

HERE'S THE SOLUTION

In this case, it's better to be safe than sorry. Give up a single to the batter. You can even give up a run. You always want to be aggressive. But in this situation, you shouldn't try for a diving catch unless you're absolutely certain you will be able to come up with the ball. Why not? Because, if the ball bounces past you, both runners will probably score and the game will be tied. The batter will get either a double or a triple, putting him in scoring position to win the game.

It's better to play it safe. Let the ball fall in for a base hit. If the runner from second is going home, don't even attempt to throw him out. Instead, throw to third base. If you do throw to home, the runner from first will probably make it to third, with the batter moving up to second base. If that happens, the tying run will be at third base and the go-ahead run will be at second. So play it safe: let the ball bounce, and then throw to third. This will most likely force the player running from first base to stop at second. Then your team is still up a run, and you also have the chance to turn a double play to get out of the jam.

Rocco Baldelli's Memories

I GREW UP in Woonsocket, Rhode Island. I played Little League with my best friend and my brother, who was two years younger than me. We were all on the same team. My dad was the coach. We played for FOP [Fraternal Order of Police] #9 in the now-defunct Fair North Little League in Woonsocket, and we had a lot of success.

I think we won our city championship two or three times, and we didn't lose a game for a couple of years. It was a lot of fun. That's where I learned basically how to play baseball. I played in my backyard and played Little League.

I pitched a lot, I caught a lot, and I played shortstop a lot. Playing in the all-stars was always a lot of fun. We went to the state tournament when I was twelve, and we were runners-up in the state. Those were good memories.

Hitting home runs was something I wanted to do, but I was more of a line-drive hitter. I did hit a bunch of homers—not sure how many, probably ten—when I was eleven and twelve. I did pretty well throwing the ball, pitched a handful of no-hitters. That kind of stuff is neat.

I enjoyed catching, too. As a catcher you're involved in every play, and you always have to be in the game.

I just remember us winning a lot of games and having fun and going to get ice cream after the game.

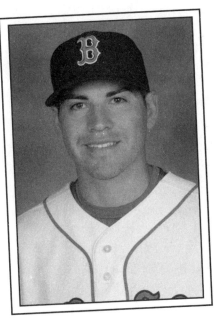

OUTFIELD THROWING

JACOBY ELLSBURY

An outfielder doesn't just catch fly balls. Although that is a major part of his job, he has to throw the ball, too. Whether the outfielder is catching a fly ball or fielding a base hit, he sometimes has an opportunity to throw out a baserunner. A chance like this often comes at an important moment in the game. Everything happens quickly, with very little margin for error.

In this chapter, Jacoby Ellsbury talks about the art of throwing out baserunners.

Are you standing still when you catch a fly ball before making a throw to a base?

No, you're not stationary when you're catching the ball in a situation like this.

127

You're not necessarily running hard and you don't have to be going fast, but you want to have the ball coming down a little in front of you as you move in with your last few steps to make the catch. That will give you a little momentum going forward as you start to throw.

Why do you need momentum going forward if you're trying to throw out a baserunner?

Let's say you're going to throw a guy out at the plate. The biggest thing is to **get behind the ball**. You want to have momentum going forward to wherever you're throwing—whether it's third, home, or second—so you have some strength behind the throw. Catching the ball with your momentum going forward will result in a harder and usually more accurate throw.

In a best-case scenario, where do you want to catch the ball if you know you have to then make a throw to a base?

I would say if you're going to make a throw, you want to catch the ball on your throwing side a little bit. So if you're right-handed, you want to catch it off to your right side of your body and if you're left-handed you want to catch it off to the left side.

Where is the bare hand as you catch the ball?

It's usually next to the glove. That helps you throw the ball quicker. With your bare hand close to the glove, you can transfer the ball from the glove to the throwing hand fast, which results in your making the throw faster. And a play like this is all about accuracy and getting rid of the ball as quickly as possible.

What is your body position when you make a throw to nail a baserunner?

You want your momentum going toward the base you're throwing to. If you are moving toward the base after fielding the ball, then your body will naturally turn in that direction and it will be lined up to make the throw. As you throw, you want to be squared up to your **target**.

Your glove-side shoulder will be pointing toward your target when you throw, but only after you have fielded the ball. As you deliver the throw, the shoulder will naturally turn to the target.

As you catch the ball, how quick do your feet have to be?

Your feet don't necessarily have to be quick, but you need the momentum going forward.

What's the technique for *charging a ground ball* and throwing to a base?

You want to get to the ball as quickly as possible, but at the same time you want to be balanced and under control so you can make an accurate throw. You can sprint in for the ball, but everything you do still has to be under control, fluid.

When reaching for the ball, what are the proper mechanics?

If the ball's hit to you in center field and you're going to throw home, you want to be **squared up** to home as you reach for the ball. Any time you make a catch, you need to be squared up with whichever base you're throwing to.

You reach down and field the ball off to your glove-hand side and then your body will naturally turn to face the object you're throwing to. Remember, though, if the ball is approaching you on your glove-hand side, you catch it, take a little **crow hop**, and throw. If the ball is approaching you on the other side, you backhand it, **plant**, and throw.

Where are your feet as you field the ground ball?

Different people teach different things. You'll see a lot of players field the ball off their front foot. If you're left-handed, the right side [glove-side] will usually be forward. Some left-handed outfielders feel more comfortable off the left leg, though. At the big league level you see guys do different things, so I would recommend you do whatever feels more comfortable.

Do you need to take a crow hop before letting the throw go?

You want to have some momentum behind the throw, but you don't want to go to an extreme, take a triple crow hop or anything like that. Just a nice crow hop, under control, is the right way to do it. First you have your momentum going forward and you reach down for the ball. After the catch you come up, take a crow hop, and make your throw with a nice follow-through. That usually results in an accurate throw.

What's the best type of grip to have on the baseball for a throw to a base?

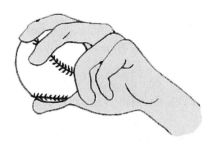

Ultimately you want the **four-seam grip** every single time when you're throwing the ball in.

Why a four-seam grip?

When you hold and throw the ball this way, you have more control, like a pitcher. You get the nice backspin and nice rotation on the ball. You don't want your throw **cutting** or **tailing**. You want it to have a nice backspin so you get the straight, ultimate distance and a **true hop**.

Does arm angle matter?

As an outfielder, you don't want to throw **sidearm** or **underhand**. You want something of an **over-the-top** delivery. Maybe not a strict over-the-top, but more like a three-quarter delivery, something between over the top and sidearm.

When you look at pitchers who throw hard, you'll see that for the most part they throw with a three-quarter delivery. As an outfielder you want to be able to throw the ball hard on a play like this. And you need to be accurate.

    **GLOSSARY**

Charging a ball: Moving forward toward the ball rather than staying in your position and waiting for the ball to come to you.

Crow hop: A quick three-part move used to get into throwing position after fielding a ground ball. The right-handed player takes a quick hop onto the right foot, then strides forward with the left, following through with a right-handed throw.

Cutting: For a left-handed thrower, throwing a ball that moves quickly from left to right; vice versa for a right-handed thrower.

Four-seam grip: A grip of the baseball in which the fingers are positioned across, not with, the four seams of the ball. This grip produces a rotation that keeps the ball moving in a straight line.

Getting behind the ball: Moving the body toward the ball as it comes down. Outfielders try to get behind the ball as they catch it in preparation for a throw to a base.

Over the top/Overhand: A throwing motion in which the arm comes up close to and past the ear when releasing the ball.

Planting: Pressing a foot into the ground.

Shortstop hole: The space on the infield dirt between the third baseman and the shortstop.

Sidearm: A throwing motion in which the arm is about waist-high and parallel to the ground upon release of the ball.

Squaring up: Turning to face the target.

Tail: The sideways movement of a ball thrown with a sidearm motion. For a right-handed thrower, the ball will "tail" from left to right as it nears the target.

Target: Where you want to throw the ball.

True hop: A predictable bounce.

Underhand: A throwing motion in which the palm of the hand faces up toward the sky. Generally a soft, but firm, toss.

His Cup Runneth Over!

When Oakland Athletics batter Johnny Damon ripped a ball down the right-field line in a game against the Boston Red Sox on August 8, 2001, it looked like a routine extra-base hit. Maybe it would be a double. Maybe the speedy Damon would even turn it into a triple.

Nothing special. Just your standard extra-base hit, right?

Wrong.

The ball bounced into the right-field corner, hitting the wall in foul territory and then ricocheting back into fair territory. But when Boston right fielder Trot Nixon went to field the ball, hoping to hold Damon to a double or throw him out at third, he suddenly became confused. The ball had disappeared. It had rolled right into a large plastic drinking cup that had fallen onto the field at some point during the inning.

Thinking quickly, Nixon held up his hand, signifying to the umpires that something out of the ordinary had happened. He figured that if he tried to shake the cup and get the ball out, Damon would easily get a triple. Maybe he would even turn the play into an inside-the-park home run. Nixon was hoping that the umpires would call it a ground-rule double, under the same ruling that applies if a ball gets stuck in the padding of a fence.

Meanwhile, Damon circled the bases, touching home plate for what he thought would be a home run. The umpires headed to right field—where Nixon was still standing looking down at the cup—to make a decision. They ruled the play a double for Damon. The

Athletics argued, figuring Damon should at least have had third base. But the argument failed.

Once the ruling had been made, Nixon picked up the cup and tried to shake out the ball. But he couldn't. It was wedged in too tightly. So he tossed the cup with the ball still inside it into the stands, giving a lucky fan an unusual souvenir.

Although Damon did not score in the inning, the Athletics eventually won the game, 6–1.

★★★★★★★★★★★★★★★★★★★★★★★★★

HERE'S THE SITUATION

The game is tied and it's the bottom of the last inning. The opposing team has a runner on second base, and there are two outs. You're playing in the outfield, and it's not as smooth a field as you might find in professional base-ball. There are plenty of bumps and divots, which keep the ball from bouncing or rolling in a nice, straight path.

The batter smacks a base hit to you. The ball is hit hard and has a lot of speed as it bounces toward you. The runner from second base is streaking around third base and heading for home, trying to score the winning run. He's a pretty fast runner.

Given the uneven conditions of the field, should you get down on one knee to make sure you at least block the ball? Or should you charge it hard?

HERE'S THE SOLUTION

Charge!

There is no alternative in this situation. You have to put a hard charge on the ball because it's your only chance to throw out the potential winning run at the plate. If you play this one safe, the runner will score easily.

If the ball gets by you or you can't field it cleanly, then that's just the way it goes. The game is over. That happens sometimes. But at least by charging the ball, you gave yourself the best chance to make the tough play.

Jacoby Ellsbury's Memories

I GREW UP in Oregon. Little League was big there.

My dad was one of the coaches when I played, so I had a good time.

I was a catcher, shortstop, and pitcher. The coaches wanted me involved in pretty much every play, so when I wasn't pitching, I was catching, and if I wasn't doing either of those two, I was playing shortstop. I didn't start playing the outfield until high school.

It wasn't that strange being a left-hander catching or playing shortstop. I made all the plays. It wasn't an issue for me throwing to first from shortstop, even from the **shortstop hole**.

As a pitcher, I had a perfect game when I was eleven or twelve. Pretty much they were all strikeouts. You know what, I think the last guy hit a little comebacker to me, and I think that might have been the only ball put in play. I could be wrong on that, but that's how I remember it.

I know I got a milk shake for every home run I hit. Not from my dad. He wouldn't buy me ice cream. He would buy me a new glove or something. One of my coaches had the idea. I think he still owes me a few milk shakes. Oh, yeah, I collected them, but I think he got tired of buying me milk shakes. In Little League I was a home-run hitter. We played maybe sixteen games, and I had something like eighteen home runs. It was fun. I enjoyed Little League.

BUNTING FOR
A BASE HIT
OR SACRIFICE

IAN KINSLER

Bunting isn't usually featured on the highlight shows every night. But while it may not pack the same punch as a home run, a well-executed bunt can prove to be a pivotal play in a team's rally. That goes for a sacrifice bunt as well as a bunt for a hit.

In this chapter, All-Star Ian Kinsler explains how to successfully drop down a bunt.

Where do you stand in the batter's box if you're going to drop down a *sacrifice bunt*?

I think the best way to do it is to scoot up as far forward in the batter's box as you can. This creates more fair territory, so you're not behind the foul line when the ball hits the bat.

Then you just want to make sure the bat is out in front of your eyes so you can see the bat make contact with the ball. You don't want the bat behind your eyes. You want it out front. And from there you just let the ball hit the bat.

Where on the bat do you want to try to hit the ball?

You try to hit it toward the end of the bat because making contact there will **deaden** the ball better. If you hit it off the barrel the ball kind of bounces off and makes an easier play for the fielder.

Do you want to reach out with the bat to get to the ball when you're bunting?

You don't want to stab at the ball. You want to basically **give with the bat** as the ball hits it and create a good angle toward the side of the field you want to bunt on, whether down the third-base line or first-base line.

At what angle should you be holding the bat? Do you totally square around at the plate, or just *pivot* the upper part of the body?

For me it's whichever way is most comfortable. I'm a right-handed hitter.

If I want to create an angle to bunt the ball toward third, I'm going to point the top of my bat at the second baseman. That way when the ball hits the bat, the angle is going to send it down toward third. If I'm going to bunt to first, I'm going to point the top of my bat at the first baseman for the angle that will send the ball toward first. Just set the angle there and move the bat up and down to where the pitch may be in order to make contact.

The bat won't be parallel to the ground for me, maybe just a little upright, maybe 10 degrees or so. Nothing drastic.

Do you move the bat up and down to account for the location of the pitch?

Well, you have to move the bat to hit the ball, but you can also move your knees and bend them to get to the ball with your bat if that's what you like to do.

I try to keep my head and my body as still as possible, so most of bunting for me is just using my arms. I try to keep my arms loose and move them up and down. When I move my bat up and down, though, I always try to keep my bat angle the same, being careful not to **drop** the barrel of the bat. If you drop the barrel of the bat, that could cause you to pop up the bunt.

Where in the strike zone do you want to have the top of the bat?

It's not a bad idea for young players to start the bat at the top of the strike zone, because, if the pitch is above the bat, it's going to be out of the strike zone and it will be called a ball. And if the pitch is above the bat and you try to bunt it, you might pop it up. So if you start with the bat at the top of the strike zone and the ball comes in higher than that, you should let it go.

I like to start with my bat in the middle of the strike zone, but I've had a lot of experience. A kid might want to stick with the top of the strike zone until they've worked on their strike-zone discipline and their ability to recognize strikes and balls.

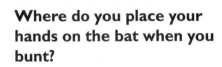

Where do you place your hands on the bat when you bunt?

I keep my bottom hand on the bottom of the bat where I normally place it to swing. I place my top hand up by the label. This method gives you the most control of the bat.

Should you wrap the fingers of the top hand around the bat?

If you need to, you can. It may be tougher for kids to do that because their hand–eye coordination is obviously not as developed, but if you feel that wrapping your fingers around the bat gives you more control of the bat, I don't see a problem with that. If you're a good bunter then it's not really a big problem. But if you have trouble bunting, or you're just learning to bunt, then I think you need to hide your fingers behind the bat.

How do you hide your fingers so they don't get hit by the pitch?

Make sure you hold the bat between your thumb and your pointer finger. Fold the rest of your fingers behind the barrel to make sure they're not exposed.

How do you bunt for a hit as a right-handed hitter?

As the ball is coming to the plate, I drop my right foot back slightly and lean over the plate a little bit. I set my angle with the bat and get it out in front of the plate. The key is to **show** it earlier than you think.

140

You don't want to show it late. A lot of guys think the later you show it, the better chance you have of a third baseman not realizing you're bunting, which gives you a better chance of **beating it out**. But I think if you get into your bunting position earlier you have a better chance of laying down a good bunt.

Plus, turning earlier slows everything down in your bunting **mechanics**. There won't be as many moving parts in your body when the ball is in the air on its way to home plate. Remember, you don't want any moving parts while the ball is in the air. You want to be ready to bunt before the pitcher lets the pitch go. And if you lay down a good bunt you should be able to beat it out.

Is the bunting technique different for a left-handed hitter?

The technique for a sacrifice is pretty similar for a left-handed hitter. There is one difference, though. If you are a left-handed batter, you can get a running start from the batter's box—get yourself moving toward first base as you bunt. This way, your time to first can be a little quicker than it is for a right-handed bunter.

GLOSSARY

Beating it out: Making it safely to the base.

Bunt field: A practice field that only has an infield, no outfield.

Deadening: Stopping the ball from bouncing or rolling.

Dropping: Lowering the bat from the angle at which it is being held.

Giving with the bat: Slightly pulling the bat back as the ball makes contact.

Mechanics: The body movements involved in playing baseball.

Pivoting: Turning or twisting your body.

Sacrifice bunt: A bunt in which the batter willingly makes an out in order to try to move the runner (or runners) up a base.

Showing it: Moving into a bunting position in the batter's box.

Then I'll Huff, and I'll Puff...

It's possible for a player to become winded every now and then. But Kansas City Royals team member Kevin Seitzer took that expression literally in a June 9, 1987, game against Minnesota.

Seitzer was playing third base. Until the eighth inning, it was a typical game. The Twins were leading 4–2, with two runners on base. Dan Gladden stepped into the batter's box to face Royals pitcher Steve Farr and decided to drop down a bunt. The ball went rolling slowly down the third-base line on the artificial turf in the Metrodome. Seitzer knew instantly he didn't have a play. Even if he charged the ball, he would have no chance to throw out Gladden. Plus, he couldn't make a play at any other base either.

In these situations, the fielder will often let the ball go, hoping it will roll into foul territory. But because they were playing on artificial turf, Seitzer knew the ball would roll on a straight path and it would stay fair.

There didn't seem to be much Seitzer could do about it. But the quick-thinking infielder made an attempt. Seitzer dropped to his knees, got his body down low to the turf, took a deep breath, and tried to blow the ball into foul territory as it continued to roll. He crawled up the baseline with the ball, his face inches from the turf, huffing and puffing the whole way—determined to blow the ball into foul territory.

It was a nice try. But apparently Seitzer wasn't a big enough windbag, because the ball stayed fair. Gladden was credited with a base hit, and the Twins ultimately scored a run later in the inning, breezing to a 5–2 win.

★ ★

HERE'S THE SITUATION

It's the last inning. Your team is losing by three runs and you're leading off. You look down the third-base line and notice that the third baseman is playing pretty deep. You're not a power hitter, though you have hit a few home runs in your career. You're very good at putting the bat on the ball and you run pretty fast.

Should you swing for the fences? Or should you try to bunt for a base hit?

HERE'S THE SOLUTION

Drop one down.

Take the chance on bunting for a base hit. Trailing by three runs, your team needs baserunners. You can't tie the game until you have two runners on base. So even if you hit a home run, your team will still be two runs down. Plus, you're more likely to make an out than hit a home run if you try to swing for the fences.

If you have speed and can make contact and the third baseman is playing deep, dropping a bunt down is a good plan. It will force the third baseman to make a tough play. And if your bunt is even halfway decent, you're likely to get on base to start a rally.

144

Ian Kinsler's Memories

IT WAS ALL baseball for me. I'm from Tucson, Arizona, and I played in a Little League called Canyon Del Oro [Canyon of Gold]. Little League was an unbelievable experience. Just everything about it. Some of my best baseball memories are from playing in that league. I would go to the park every night, even if my team didn't have a game. I chased foul balls. We had water fights.

We had a little **bunt field** behind the main "Majors field." We'd get four guys together and play bunt ball, wall ball, and tag. We were always playing a game, running around. If I finished my homework I was allowed to go up there, so that was my goal every night.

Every Sunday my dad would get as many kids together as he could and we'd go to the field. We'd practice and play and throw and take ground balls. That was a lot of fun. Just a moment in time when you don't know anything about baseball and you're just playing it because you love it. You're playing it because you're a natural at it, good at it. No one's trying to feed you information about the right or the wrong way to play, you're just doing things with natural ability. That's why I think I loved it so much.

I was on the Cubs, sponsored by Mama's Pizza. I was a shortstop and I pitched. I was good at pitching, but when I was

145

twelve my dad made me choose between being a position player or a pitcher. He didn't want me to do both, so obviously I chose to play in the field and hit because I loved hitting.

Pitching was fun while I did it. I didn't know anything about it. I was never taught mechanics. I just basically reached back to the center field wall, picked my leg up as high as I could and chucked it.

I hit a home run left-handed one time. My dad was a switch-hitter so I wanted to be a switch-hitter, too. He let me switch-hit if we were losing by a lot or winning by a lot. I got a couple of left-handed at-bats and I was able to hit one out, which was pretty cool. It surprised me a little bit. I thought I was pretty good at switch-hitting, but I never thought I'd be able to hit a home run. I think a lot of it was luck. My dad wanted me to take as many swings left-handed as I did right-handed if I wanted to switch hit. I wasn't up to that so I let the switch-hitting thing go.

BASIC HITTING FUNDAMENTALS

JOE MAUER

Some people say that the most difficult task in all of sports is trying to hit a round ball squarely with a round bat. If the ball isn't hit squarely, it isn't likely to travel very far, nor will it be hit very hard. So it's important to keep your eye on the ball.

In this chapter, American League MVP, batting champion, and All-Star Joe Mauer offers a few suggestions on how to see and hit the ball.

What is one of the most important qualities that a good hitter has to have?

I think one of the keys is balance. When you get a little older and pitchers start to change speeds more often, balance is very important for a hitter.

You want to stay under control in the batter's box. If you're all timed to hit a fastball and someone throws you a **changeup**, you'll end up way out on your front foot when you make contact with the ball. And when that happens, you lose a lot of your power.

Are there any other reasons why balance in the batter's box is important?

It's also important to stay balanced because after you hit the ball you have to run. You don't want to be falling over or leaning to one side or another after you've made contact because then you won't be able to get a good, quick start toward first base.

Is there one type of stance that works best for a good hitter?

If you look at a lot of big league hitters you'll see a lot of different stances, different ways in which they get their timing at the plate.

But your hands always have to be in a good position the moment you begin to swing at the ball. The most direct movement of the hands to the ball starts with your hands coming from near your back shoulder. There are a lot of ways to get to that point. Some guys may start in their stance with their hands held high, and others may start with their hands down low. But every hitter begins a swing with the hands at the back shoulder because that's the most direct way to the ball.

Do you want your head to be moving as you try to hit the ball?

I always try to keep my head still so I can keep my eyes on the ball.

It's like when you're trying to catch a pop fly in the outfield. If you run and your head is bouncing up and down, it's going to make it look like the ball is bouncing up and down in the air, which makes it harder to see and to catch.

148

At the plate, if your head isn't still, an incoming pitch is going to look like it's moving and it will be tougher to see. I want to be able to **track** the ball as closely as I can. Holding my head still helps me look for a pitch I can handle and hit hard.

Are there any types of drills that kids can do to help them keep their eyes on the ball?

Bunting can help.

A lot of times, even now that I'm in the big leagues, if I don't feel like I'm seeing the ball real well, I'll go down to the batting cage and bunt pitches. That helps me track the ball. When I'm bunting, I can almost see the ball hit the bat, so there are times when I bunt a lot before batting practice.

Should young players try to hit home runs?

I don't think so. I usually hit home runs when I'm not even trying to. My approach is just to hit the ball hard somewhere. If you do that, sometimes the ball is going to fly over the fence. When I try to hit a home run, my swing gets too long and sometimes I'm late swinging at the pitch.

You mean you don't have to swing from as far back as you can, as hard as you can in order to hit the ball deep?

There's one thing about hitting that I still believe in: you have to have a short, compact swing.

You want to be under control at the plate with your swing. A powerful swing doesn't have to be a long one. You can still generate a lot of power with a short, quick swing.

When you see a good pitch coming to the plate, one you know you can hit, do you want to jump at the ball?

When the pitch comes in I want to have a little momentum, a little movement going forward, but I still want to be balanced and I want to **stay back on the ball**.

When you jump out at the ball, it makes it look like the ball is coming in even faster, and that makes it harder to hit well. And if the pitch happens to be a changeup and you jump at the ball, you'll be off balance. You definitely don't want to jump at the ball.

    GLOSSARY

Changeup: A pitch that is meant to look like a fastball when it leaves the pitcher's hand but in fact arrives at the plate at a slower speed.

Staying back on the ball: Keeping your body in a balanced, ready-to-hit position for as long as possible before swinging, which gives you a better chance to hit the ball well.

Tracking: Watching closely.

The Eyes Have It!

Wade Boggs had one of the best batting eyes in the history of the Major Leagues. Not only did he use his keen eyesight to notch 3,010 hits, but he also drew 1,412 walks in his 2,440-game career. No one watched the ball all the way into the catcher's mitt better than Boggs. He refused to swing unless he saw a pitch he thought he could hit well.

And in Game 4 of the 1996 World Series, Boggs's patience paid off.

The game was tied at 6–6, heading into the tenth inning. When Wade Boggs stepped to the plate, there were two outs and the bases were loaded with Yankees. Boggs fell behind in the count 1–2, then took some close pitches that were called balls. Finally, on a 3-and-2 pitch, Boggs took another close pitch, which was also called a ball. He had earned a walk, and the tie-breaking run was forced in. The Yankees went on to win the game—and eventually, the 1996 World Series!

HERE'S THE SITUATION

The pitcher you're facing is a little wild. He has walked the last two batters and thrown just one strike out of his last nine pitches. There are runners at first and second, with no one out. It's the third inning and your team is behind by five runs. It's your turn to hit. You step in the batter's box and swing your bat back and forth, getting ready for the first pitch.

Should you swing at that first pitch, guessing that the pitcher is due to throw a strike?

HERE'S THE SOLUTION

It might be a good idea to take the first pitch, even if it turns out to be a strike. Clearly, the pitcher is struggling. You're down by five runs, so the more runners you can get on base, the quicker you'll have an opportunity to catch up.

It's okay if that first pitch turns out to be a strike. The pressure is still on the pitcher. If he's wild, there are good odds that he's just trying to throw a strike and not worrying too much about how hard the ball is thrown. If you have confidence in yourself as a hitter, you'll be ready if the pitcher is able to throw his next pitch for a strike. Besides, taking a pitch every now and then can help you practice watching the ball all the way into the catcher's mitt.

If the first two pitches are out of the strike zone, you might want to consider taking more pitches until this pitcher proves he can throw a strike. Even a walk in this situation would be helpful to your team because it would load the bases and keep the rally going.

Joe Mauer's Memories

I GREW UP in St. Paul, Minnesota. I played on a lot of teams, like teams at recreation centers—as many as they would let me play on.

We played in a lot of weekend tournaments, maybe five or six games a weekend. I had a lot of fun doing it.

I played all over—shortstop, catcher, third base, pitcher, outfielder, and first base. I don't know that I was much of a pitcher. I just threw the ball. I could always throw harder than most of the other kids, and I threw a pretty straight fastball. I might have hit a few more home runs then than I do now. I've hit third in the batting order all my life.

I had really good coaches. If we threw a helmet or a bat, the coaches were quick to get on us and tell us that wasn't the right way to play. And they were right. I never was someone who threw the helmet much.

THE POWER STROKE

RYAN HOWARD

As a hitter, there is nothing more exciting than crushing a baseball with a good swing and sending it flying over the fence. The home-run trot that follows is as good as it gets! Sheer strength can be helpful in hitting home runs. But it isn't just the biggest and strongest batters who hit the ball out of the park.

In this chapter, National League MVP, Rookie of the Year, and All-Star home-run champion Ryan Howard analyzes techniques to help a batter hit for power.

Is there one aspect of being able to hit for power that's more important than any other?

Some people may be larger or they may just be stronger than others. If you had to identify one thing, it could be strength. A lot of strength, though, is all about using correct **mechanics** and good technique during your swing and your approach. You don't have to be large to hit home runs.

Is hitting for power just a function of having strong arms?

No, no, no, no.

I mean, any type of hitting starts with the bottom half of your body. It starts with your **stance**. That's your foundation.

Think of it this way—if the foundation of a building is weak, that building is going to crumble. It's the same with hitting. As long as you have a strong base, a stable base, and you are balanced at all points through your swing, your swing is going to be strong.

Do you want to be flat-footed in your stance or on the balls of your feet?

It varies with everybody. Some people can stand flat-footed, but I think at some point, once you actually get into your hitting motion, you'll wind up on the balls of your feet because you have to make the transfer of your weight from the back side to the front side as you start your swing. You can't really do that if you're flat-footed and on your heels.

As long as you can get that weight transferred to the balls of your feet, so that when you go to swing you will be transferring your weight forward through the ball, then you're good to go.

Why is the shift of your weight important?

As you shift your weight, you create momentum. That's basically what you're trying to hit the ball with, that momentum. You can't stay on your back side and swing kind of flat. You want your entire body to get into the swing, but you also want to make it as smooth as possible so you can hit the ball hard and generate power.

How important are the hands in power hitting?

Every aspect of the swing is important in its own right. The hands are important in many ways, from placing them in the right spot to grip the bat all the way down to having them in the right motion as you swing so you can bring your hands through the **zone** the proper way.

Why is bat speed important?

Bat speed is important because that's how you get to the ball with your swing.

If you have a pitcher who's throwing really hard, maybe 95 to 100 miles an hour in the big leagues, you definitely need bat speed. Or, if you have a guy with a very slow curveball, your bat speed allows you to wait that much longer to hit that pitch. You can wait for the ball to get to the plate and you'll still be able to snap the bat through the zone and drive it.

Is there one perfect angle of the bat that's most likely to allow you to drive the ball with power?

It's a personal preference, but if you do try to take a **line-drive approach** at the plate, you want to create **backspin** on the ball when you hit it. When you have that backspin on the ball after you hit it, the ball will take off. And as it goes through the infield and the outfield it will continue to rise and go out of the ballpark.

If you try to hit home runs with an **uppercut swing** you have to be pretty much perfect every time. You'd have to hit the ball in the right spot at the right time to be able to lift through it to hit it over the fence. If you don't hit it just right with the uppercut swing, you'll hit the ball with a lot of **topspin** so it will go up and then come right back down, or you may **roll over** on the ball and hit a dribbler to second or short.

Is it best to keep both hands on the bat as you swing through the zone, or is it best to take one hand off?

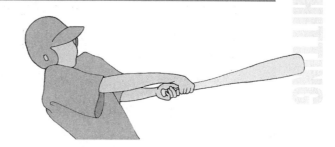

That's personal preference, too.

Usually they'll tell guys like myself, bigger and taller guys, that you should come through the zone with two hands on the bat, and then do a one-hand release after contact on the follow-through so you can feel more free, more fluid. The smaller **contact-type hitters** tend to keep two hands on the bat.

Do you get more extension with the bat when you take one hand off it, generating more power in the process?

I think you do feel that way, but either approach can work. When you get to the ball in your swing—when you're about to hit it—your hands are still bent, and then you pull them through as you hit it. And when the ball is already gone off the bat, that's when you let go of the bat with your top hand.

How difficult is it to hit a home run when you're trying to?

That's not something you even try to do. I mean, if you could hit a home run on demand any time you wanted to, you'd be the greatest player ever.

Can you get into bad habits if you try to hit the ball too hard and too far?

If you try and hit home runs like that, you do develop bad habits. You can get a bad uppercut in your swing. You might end up with a slow bat because you're trying to swing too hard.

Maybe then you start pulling your head out so soon that you don't even see the ball, and your front shoulder is **pulling off the ball**. Your front shoulder needs to stay in and your head needs to stay down so you can see the ball.

Should your head be still during the swing?

Yes. You want to try and keep it as still as possible, because once your head is moving—and remember, the ball is moving, too—it is much more difficult to hit the ball squarely. If your head is moving, you're going to miss the ball or mis-hit it a majority of the time.

When you step in the batter's box, what are you looking at?

You try to pick up the **release point**. Once the ball leaves the pitcher's hand, you want to track it as long as you can.

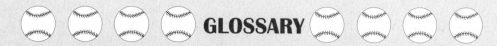 **GLOSSARY**

Backspin: The backward rotation of a ball.

Contact-type hitter: A hitter who tends to just make contact with the ball and doesn't hit for power.

Line-drive approach: A method of hitting that employs a basically level swing, designed to produce line drives.

Mechanics: The body movements involved in playing baseball.

Pulling off the ball: Moving the body away from the pitch as it nears the plate.

Release point: The spot where the ball leaves the pitcher's hand on its way to the plate.

Rolling over: Moving your arms during a swing so that the top wrist rolls over the bottom wrist on contact; this generally leads to a weak ground ball.

Stance: A player's body position.

Topspin: The forward rotation of a ball.

Uppercut swing: A swing in which the bat starts low and finishes high.

Zone: The area in which a ball arrives at home plate. It usually refers to the strike zone, where a pitch would be called a strike if the hitter let it go by.

Three Cheers for the Powerful Little Guy!

It's not unheard of for a player to hit three home runs a game. Generally, such power displays are reserved for the biggest sluggers in the majors.

However, Freddie Patek accomplished the same feat in 1980. Patek was a small infielder, standing about 5'5" and weighing a mere 148 pounds. He was better known for his defensive abilities in his fourteen big league seasons, rather than his home-run hitting ability. In fact, in his 1,650 major league games, Patek hit a total of forty-one home runs.

But on June 20, 1980, Patek launched three home runs out of Boston's Fenway Park, leading the California Angels to a 20–2 rout of the Red Sox. Patek, who also had a double in the game, hit solo, two-run, and three-run homers.

Patek only hit two other homers for the rest of the year. He finished the season with a total of five. And he never hit more than six home runs in any of his other major league seasons. But on that one night, Freddie Patek showed the baseball world that hitting home runs was not strictly for the big guys.

★ ★

HERE'S THE SITUATION

There are two runners on base when you step into the batter's box. The game is tied up in the later innings. The count is 2 and 0. The next pitch is on the outside corner, about knee-high. It's a borderline strike. Maybe it will be called a strike, but there's a chance that it could also be called a ball.

Should you swing?

HERE'S THE SOLUTION

Take the pitch.

When the count is 2–0, or even 3–1, those are called hitter's counts. This means that the hitter can be selective about which pitches he chooses to swing at. When a hitter is ahead in the count, there's no need to swing at a tough pitch... even if it's a strike. The odds of squarely hitting a tough pitch are not good, so there's no reason to help out the pitcher.

So take the tough pitch. Even if it's called a strike, the pitcher still has to throw a strike on his next pitch at 2–1 or 3–2. And it's not that easy for a pitcher to make two tough pitches in a row. The odds are in your favor that the next pitch will be a good one to hit.

Of course, taking a pitch requires discipline at the plate. If you see a pitch you think you can hit, you may immediately want to swing at it. But if you have confidence as a hitter, you also know you can wait for the better pitch.

Ryan Howard's Memories

I GREW UP in St. Louis, Missouri. I remember hot summers, July and August, crazy hot. But, man, it was so much fun playing baseball. I remember the smell of the grass, being out there on the field with my friends, just running around and enjoying the game.

Around the time I was eight to twelve years old I played first base and some outfield.

We played in a lot of different tournaments. It was exciting for me when we got to go to tournaments because we were going to new towns, and it was great to experience new places, playing on new fields against different teams from across the country. That was pretty cool. We used to travel with people's parents driving carpools in caravans.

We used to go to Memphis a lot, which was around five hours away. There was a Fourth of July tournament down there. They had this club team called the Memphis Tigers, and we played in their tournament. Then they'd come up and play in our tournament in St. Louis.

Those were good games because those teams were pretty good. I think I hit three or four homers against them. I was probably a little bit taller than everyone else.

We were part of the Ballwin Athletic Association. I played for teams named the Warriors, the Giants, the Royals. After the games were over we'd run to the concessions stand and grab some fries and something to drink and then just head home.

The fields were good. There was a big field, a Legion field, with big league measurements. That was Field 1, and that one had grass in the infield. Then there were other age-appropriate-sized fields. The rest were all dirt infields, which was pretty rough at first base.

THE ART OF CLUTCH HITTING

JASON BAY

As a hitter, you feel the pressure each time you step into the batter's box. There's no one to help you out—it's just you and the pitcher. But the pressure level rises when there are runners on base in a tight game and you're the one up at bat. Your teammates are counting on you to come through to help win the game. The butterflies are dancing in your stomach. It's not at all unusual for a batter to be nervous in this important situation.

In this chapter, National League Rookie of the Year and All-Star Jason Bay talks about how to conquer nerves and turn that energy into a positive and productive at bat.

In that key moment late in the game, with runners in scoring position, is the pressure on the pitcher or the hitter?

I think it's on the pitcher.

He has to throw some strikes. As a hitter, I think the biggest thing is that you have to go up to the plate with the mentality that even though it's a clutch situation, you need to approach it the same way you do every at bat. When you start doing things differently, that's when you get out of your comfort zone.

In your mind, you don't want to make it a bigger situation than it already is. Don't tell yourself that you have to do something. Any time you start saying, "I have to do something," you get into trouble because you put too much pressure on yourself.

Because the pressure is on the pitcher to throw strikes, do you go to the plate expecting a pitch down the middle?

The pitcher wants to make sure he throws a strike right away and then he can relax a little bit. So as a hitter you have to be ready for that. But you don't want to swing at the first pitch just because you know the pitcher is trying to throw a strike on that pitch. You get three strikes, so if that first pitch isn't the one you want, you wait him out and try to get one that's yours. Wait for a pitch that's better for you to swing at and hit hard.

Some guys get a little too excited. They want to get that big hit so badly they might swing early in the **count** at a pitch they shouldn't swing at. Even if it is a strike, it may not be a pitch you can do a lot with. Patience to wait for their pitch makes certain people better in the clutch.

How much does your concentration change in a late-game pressure situation?

I don't think it should.

Sometimes in those situations you have a little extra incentive and things are a little clearer or crisper in your mind. But you should always go up to the plate with a plan. "I want to do this with a certain type of pitch in a certain location," or, "I don't want to swing at the first pitch." You have to have some kind of plan. You can't go up there blind, so to speak.

That's what makes a good clutch hitter, being able to stick to your plan in a pressure situation, especially late in the game.

Can you learn anything by watching the pitcher warming up or during the inning against other hitters?

You should watch the pitcher warm up. If a player sees the pitcher throw eight balls to the **backstop** during warm-ups and then goes up and swings at the first pitch and it wasn't close to the strike zone, then he wasn't really learning anything as he watched. You need to pay attention. Little things like that can make a big difference.

But if another player saw that the pitcher wasn't throwing strikes during warm-ups and decided that maybe **taking a pitch** would be a good idea, then he has learned something from watching. When you pay close attention to what a pitcher is doing and then come up with a good plan, you should stick with it.

Do you swing for home runs in clutch situations?

That's an easy question for me to answer because I don't.

I hit home runs, but I don't consider myself to be a home-run hitter. I'm a pretty classic example of the fact that home runs just happen if you hit the ball hard. Sometimes they go out.

Some guys can swing for home runs and hit them, but those guys are special talents. For most of us, when you try to hit home runs, you end up doing a lot of things wrong. You **step in the bucket**, your swing gets long, or you try too hard.

On the other hand, when you just try to hit the ball **up the middle**, that's when everything stays where it's supposed to in your swing, and sometimes you find one in the right spot and hit a home run. I think it's a lot easier to approach every at bat that way.

There is pressure on a hitter, too. How does a hitter calm down in stressful situations?

It's not easy, especially if you haven't gone through the situation a lot. Any time you have past experiences it helps, because the unknown is usually worse and seems more difficult than the actual act.

The first time somebody comes up in a big situation he's going to be nervous. That still makes me nervous, and I'm thirty years old and have done it so many times. But gradually you learn, through experience, how you will react to the pressure. That knowledge is important and helps to control your nerves. Now, I just take a deep breath and exhale slowly. That's where I start before I get into the batter's box. For me that's relaxing and turns my nervousness into concentration. I tell myself, "Hey, it's just another at bat."

Do you try to forget there are runners on base?

For me, having runners on base is like having people in the stands. There may be a lot going on in the stadium, but I don't even hear the fans. When I'm up and there are runners on base, I'm not thinking about them. I'm just trying to do my job. I'm not trying to hit a home run. I'm not trying to do too much. I'm just trying to get on base.

After you've done it enough times and had some success, you just know what you want to do at the plate. You get so involved and so focused on doing what you want to do that everything else fades out. It's like tunnel vision.

This concentration is not something that comes right away. It comes through experience. If at first you get a little overwhelmed or a little nervous in those situations, that's completely normal. Everyone has been like that at some point. But every at bat, if you are paying attention, is preparing you to be a better hitter, no matter the pressure.

GLOSSARY

Backstop: The fence behind home plate.

Count: The number of balls and strikes the batter has on him at any given time during an at bat. For instance, the count may be two balls and no strikes. Or it could be three balls and two strikes, which is called a "full" count.

Stepping in the bucket: Taking a step away from the plate with the front foot as the pitch approaches. This makes it more difficult for the hitter to reach the ball.

Taking a pitch: Watching a pitch go by with no intention of swinging at it.

Up the middle: The area in the middle of the baseball diamond—through the pitcher's mound, past second base, and into center field.

Armed and Dangerous— or a Real Corker?

Albert Belle already had a reputation as one of the most powerful hitters in the game when he stepped to the plate in the eleventh inning of Game 1 of the American League Divisional playoffs. The Boston Red Sox were leading, 4–3 on October 3, 1995, at Cleveland's Jacobs Field.

But the lead didn't last long. Belle crushed a home run to left field off Rick Aguilera, tying the game at 4–4 and setting off stadium fireworks. However, Red Sox manager Kevin Kennedy suspected that Belle, who had hit fifty homers that season, was using a corked bat. So Kennedy demanded that the home-plate umpire take the bat for further examination. If the bat had been corked, Belle would have been fined and suspended.

A corked bat is a bat that has been hollowed out from the top of the barrel down toward the label. The missing wood is replaced with cork, which is lighter and helps a batter swing the bat faster, generating more power than usual. In the Major Leagues, it is illegal to use a corked bat.

Belle's bat was sent to the umpire's room. Belle was absolutely furious. From the Cleveland dugout, he pulled up the right sleeve of his jersey and flexed his large biceps at Kennedy. He pointed at it and yelled that with his strength, he didn't need any illegal help.

The game eventually continued and the Indians won, 5–4. Cleveland ultimately swept the series in three games. Belle's bat was x-rayed, and found not to have been corked.

But a few years later, the full story came out.

Jason Grimsley, a pitcher for Cleveland in 1995, came clean four years later, when he was pitching for the New York Yankees. He said he knew that Belle's bat was corked, so he climbed through a heating duct in the roof of the stadium and found his way into the umpires' room. He then exchanged a non-corked bat for the corked one without anyone seeing him. That's why the x-rays showed nothing but a regular bat.

Unfortunately for the Red Sox, Grimsley's confession came four years too late.

HERE'S THE SITUATION

The bases are loaded, there are two outs, and your team is two runs behind in the final inning. All kinds of questions are running through your mind.

Should you swing for the fences? Try to hit a grand slam? Should you swing as hard as you can? Should you swing if the ball is close to the plate, even if it's not a strike?

HERE'S THE SOLUTION

Relax.

Although it may be easier said than done, you should treat this at-bat as you would any other. You only want to swing at strikes. If the pitcher doesn't throw strikes, he'll walk you and force in a run. But you must always be ready for a strike. And if he throws one, take your normal swing. That's the best you can do. Wait for a good pitch and then try to hit it squarely with your best swing.

Jason Bay's Memories

I WENT to the Little League World Series when I was eleven, representing Team Canada.

Back then I was small. I was really fast, so I played center field, batted second, bunted, and stole a lot because I had the wheels. We had a lot of guys behind me in the order who could hit.

Growing up in Trail, British Columbia, a town of just under 8,000 people, we played in front of 50 parents. Then we went to the regionals and played in front of 100 to 300 people, and then suddenly we were playing in front of 10,000 people in a stadium in Williamsport, Pennsylvania! I had never played in a stadium before. Where I grew up, all the fields had chain-link fences and small bleachers.

I was a little overwhelmed and definitely nervous playing against the best in the world. But once the game started and we got into it, hey, it was just another Little League game. Playing in the Little League World Series was probably one of the biggest steps in my baseball career.

Back then it was a single-elimination tournament. We beat a team from Mexico, 8–3, which put us in the foreign finals because in those years there were only four United States teams and four foreign teams. Then we got crushed by Chinese Taipei, 20–1. That was the only game we lost all year.

It was pretty amazing, and it was probably easier to stomach a 20–1 loss than to have the rug pulled out from you in the last inning. It was 4–0 after the first inning, then 8–1, 12–1. So the writing was on the wall. I scored our only run. I bunted for a hit, went to second on a wild pitch, and scored on a single. That was the only run they gave up the whole tournament.

The stereotype is that Canadians play hockey, and I played hockey until I was twelve or thirteen years old. That's what you did in the winter in small towns in Canada, and in the summer you played baseball. There weren't a lot of options.

In baseball, I couldn't wait to go to the games. I would go hours early. Also, I would play catch with my dad in the back-yard all the time. Hockey was more of a grind for me. So when I finally got to the age of twelve, my parents said I didn't have to play hockey and I said, "I don't?"

They said, "No."

I said, "You wouldn't be mad?"

They said "No." I didn't have the same passion for hockey that I had for baseball. I was doing it just to do it. But I loved baseball.

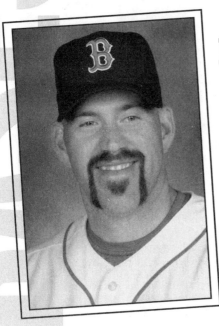

RUNDOWNS

KEVIN YOUKILIS

T he runner is trapped between bases. His chances for survival are slim. But he doesn't give up. He keeps running back and forth between the bases, trying to avoid being tagged. He's in a situation commonly referred to as "being in a **pickle**."

In this chapter, All-Star infielder Kevin Youkilis discusses how to make sure the runner doesn't make it safely out of the pickle.

Let's say you're the third baseman and the runner is trapped between second base and third base and you have the ball. What do you do?

If the runner's coming toward you, the biggest thing is you want to run the guy back (to second base) as hard as you can and get him going full speed. Then you give the ball up just in time, so it's not exactly where the second baseman or shortstop has to tag the runner, but more or less in a place where your teammate can catch the ball and then take a step and tag him out.

Why do you want to run him back to the base he came from?

Well, it doesn't really matter which base you get him going to. You just want to be sure to get the out. You don't want the runner to be able to advance a base. You want to run him back as hard as you can to get him going as fast as possible so he can't stop in the **basepath**. If he's running at full speed it's hard for him to stop and change direction and come back the other way.

Where do you want to be standing if you're participating in a rundown?

You want to make sure both fielders are on the same side of the basepath. If the shortstop or second baseman is on the **inside of the basepath**, then you want to be on the inside. If the guy running with the ball during the rundown is on the **outside of the basepath**, the other fielder has to be on the outside. You don't want to be in a situation where you're throwing the ball from the inside of the basepath to the outside, because then you might hit the runner with the ball, and you won't be able to get him out.

When you're chasing the runner, where is the ball?

Always in your bare hand. You don't **pump fake**, you just run and make a quick flip with your bare hand.

175

Why would you not want to pump fake with the ball? Wouldn't that confuse the runner and maybe make him stop in the basepath so he'd be easier to tag out?

The problem when you pump fake is you fake out the second baseman or shortstop at the other end of the rundown, and they get back on their heels and have a harder time reacting to the throw when you finally make it. So you want to hold the ball in your bare hand and run with it. Then you can just flip it to your teammate, and he'll be ready for it.

Where do you hold the ball when you're chasing the runner?

You hold it up high, from where you can make a quick throw.

Why don't you want to hold the ball in the glove during a rundown?

If you have the ball in your glove, you might drop it when you're transferring it from the glove to your hand to make a throw. It takes longer to transfer the ball from your glove to your hand and then throw it, so you would lose some time, too.

If you have gotten close enough to a runner in a rundown to tag him, do you want to tag him with the ball in your bare hand or in the glove?

Basically when you go to tag him, you want to do it any way you can. But you have to make sure you can hold onto the ball. If you can tag him with two hands that's probably the best way to do it because the ball is more protected, safer from being dropped or knocked out of your hand.

But you do whatever you have to do. Sometimes you've got to improvise—dive or do something crazy like that.

176

What type of throw do you make to the fielder at the other end of the rundown?

It's just a quick little toss. It doesn't have to be hard, just a little flick, throwing the ball **on a line**.

When the second baseman has the ball and is running toward you at third base with the runner trapped in between, where do you position yourself to receive the throw? At the third-base bag?

On this play you start short of the bag because you want to close the gap [between the infielders involved]. You don't want to give the runner a lot of room to run, to stop and change directions, to keep the rundown going. But you don't want to get too close, either. You want to be maybe ten feet off the base and then slowly move toward the runner, not walking but slowly running under control.

And if the guy on the other end of the rundown is running on the inside, you want to

make sure you're on the inside, too. That way you'll be in plain view where he can toss the ball to you easily.

How many throws should it take to put out a runner in a well-executed rundown?

Well, the goal is one. But the ultimate goal is to get an out on the play any way you can, so if it takes ten throws, it takes ten. One throw is the best-case scenario, but even if it takes a hundred throws, as long as you get the guy out, it's worth hanging in there. It's all about getting the out.

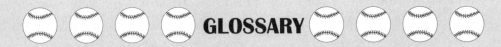

GLOSSARY

Basepath: The area within which a baserunner must stay when running between bases.

Inside of the basepath: The part of the basepath that is closer to the infield grass and pitcher's mound.

On a line: Term used to describe a throw that has no arc to it.

Outside of the basepath: The part of the basepath that is closer to the outfield grass.

Pickle: A rundown, or when a runner is trapped between bases.

Pivoting: Turning or twisting your body.

Pump faking: Pretending to throw the ball.

The Sacrifice Thigh

During the 1978 World Series, the New York Yankees' Reggie Jackson was involved in a controversial play.

Jackson was on first base when a soft, low liner was hit up the middle. The Los Angeles Dodgers shortstop, Bill Russell, came racing in to make the play. Jackson wasn't sure if Russell would catch the ball in the air, or if it would hit the ground first. This caused Jackson some baserunning indecision. He started off first, then went back.

Russell, meanwhile, trapped the ball on one short hop. He didn't catch it in the air. He stepped on second base for a forceout. But when he threw to first for the double play, Jackson was in the baseline and the throw hit him on the thigh. The batter was safe at first. The Dodgers argued that Jackson had stuck his thigh out on purpose and therefore should have been called for interference. But the umpire didn't see it that way. No interference was called and the batter was safe at first.

Unfortunately for the Dodgers, that call wasn't the only thing to go New York's way. The Yankees won the Series, 4 games to 2.

HERE'S THE SITUATION

Runners are at first and third and there are two outs. Your team is ahead by a run, and it's the last inning. You're playing shortstop. The runner from first base takes off for second, trying to steal the bag. You cover second and take a good throw from the catcher. But the runner doesn't continue all the way to second. He gets in a rundown, trying to create enough confusion so the runner from third can sneak home and tie the game.

What do you do?

HERE'S THE SOLUTION

Start chasing the runner back to first base. At the same time, peek over toward third base to see what the runner there is doing. If the third-base runner breaks for the plate, quickly **pivot** and throw home. If he scores, the game will tied, so you want to make sure he doesn't score. But if he doesn't break toward home, continue to chase the first-base runner until you can apply the tag or throw the ball to the first baseman so he can do so.

Kevin Youkilis's Memories

I GREW UP in Cincinnati, Ohio, and when I was between eight and twelve, I played Knothole Baseball, and I played a little bit in the Select Baseball League when I was eleven. Growing up that's all I did in the summertime, played Knothole Baseball.

I played a bunch of different positions—shortstop, outfield one year when I was eleven, third base, and I also pitched. I did it all. I was always a good hitter. All of us in the big leagues were good hitters when we were younger. Most of the guys in the big leagues were the best Little Leaguers in their areas when they were growing up.

We had the same Rawlings-type gloves, and Mizuno batting gloves were big back then, the kind Rickey Henderson wore. We used the metal bats called Bombats. Not anything fancy.

Basically, it was all baseball for me. I used to get upset when games got rained out. I just loved going to play baseball on Saturday mornings, or whatever day we had a game. It was just fun to wake up and go and play baseball and play competitively. I was always very competitive. I liked winning and doing well.

Our Select team traveled all over Ohio, Indiana, Kentucky, and then we went to Iowa for a World Series when I was eleven.

RUNNING THE BASES

CARL CRAWFORD

How hard can running the bases be? You hit the pitch and race to first base as fast as you can. Then it's on to second base, third base, and then home plate. But it's a lot more complicated than it seems. Being able to run fast is a big plus, but baserunning is not just about speed. There's much more to it.

In this chapter, All-Star Carl Crawford, one of the game's best baserunners, offers some helpful hints for use on the basepaths.

After you have hit the ball, what's the first thing you do?

The first thing I do is run out of the batter's box as fast as I can.

Suppose it's a routine ground ball to the infield, a seemingly certain "out." Do you stop running as you get to first base?

On a routine ground ball you still want to run hard. You never know. The fielder might bobble the ball, so you want to break out of the box as hard as you can.

And you want to **run through the bag**. You don't want to slow down and just stop when you get to the bag. You might have a chance of **beating it out** for a hit, so you want to keep running hard when you touch the bag. You slow down after you've gone past the bag.

Do you take a peek at the ball and where it's going after you have hit it?

No, you don't want to watch the ball at all. You're just focusing on getting to the bag as fast as you can.

If you look at the ball, you're going to have to turn your head to the left or the right and that's probably going to slow you down a little bit. It's like running track—you want to just run and look straight ahead. That gives you the best chance of reaching the base safely.

Suppose you get a base hit to left field, and you know it's going to fall in safely. What do you do when you get close to the first-base bag?

First of all, even if you know the ball is going to drop in, in your mind you want to assume it's going to be a double and not just a single, so you're running hard right out of the batter's box. If you don't run hard right away, you might lose your chance to get that extra base and turn the hit into a double.

Then, when you get near first base you want to round the bag nicely so you can get a good angle toward second base. You want to step on the inside [left] corner of the bag, which will help push you toward second base. After you make the turn at the bag, you look up to see what's going on. If the outfielder has the ball, you stop and come back to first with a single. If you see him bobble the ball or see that he's backhanding it and you think you can make it to second, you keep going.

But you definitely have to be thinking "two" right out of the box.

Do you run in a straight line to first base in this situation?

I run down the line with, like, a little **banana curve** so I can get a good angle toward second base. I'll move a little to my right as I run down the first-base line and bend back toward the inside of the first-base bag so I can have some momentum going to second when I hit the corner of the first-base bag.

With which foot do you hit first base as you round it?

I usually hit it with my inside [left] foot. But I don't think it really matters. I use that leg because it's my stronger leg and I can push off on it the hardest and it gets me going forward better.

How do you slide if, for instance, you're going for a double?

I never slide headfirst because I like to avoid injury. You can get hurt with your fingers and hands out there like that. I definitely slide feet first, on my left side. You kind of know when to slide by feel. You don't want to slide too soon or too late. If you slide too late you might get hurt, jamming your leg into the base. If you slide too soon, you might not get to the base and you'll be out.

If you're running from first base and the batter gets a hit to right-center, what are you looking at? The ball? The third-base coach?

First of all, before the pitch and before the play even happens, you look to see where the outfielders are standing. So, for instance, if they're playing back deep, you are aware if the ball is hit softly to them, you'll be mentally prepared to go from first to third on the hit. It's kind of like thinking about that double right out of the box.

So you round the second-base bag hard and then you **pick up** your third-base coach as you come around second. And if you're running hard enough and he thinks you can make it to third, he'll wave you over. If not, he'll give you the stop sign.

How do you run from first when there's a ball hit deep into the *gap*?

You still want to pick up your base coach, but in the back of your mind you know you're running hard and you want to give yourself every opportunity to be able to score from first on that ball when it's in the gap.

I take a lot of pride in trying to go from first to home. It's all about getting a good **jump** off the bag, a **good read** on where the ball is going to go, and running hard to make it easier for the third-base coach to decide whether to send you home.

When you're running from first to third, how do you turn the bases?

You want to get the same angle that you have when you're going from home to second. You want to get that inside foot on the inside corner of the bag and take up as little space as possible, not running wide around the bases.

How do you round third with a chance to score?

You don't want too much of a banana curve coming around third base because you don't have any time to waste. If you round it too far, too wide, that can result in a **bang-bang play** at home plate, a close matter of being out or safe.

So you want to cut down on some of that distance around the bag, which can probably get you home safely if there's a bang-bang play. Every step and every second can be important.

What do you do as a baserunner if you get caught in a rundown between second and third, for instance, with another runner behind you and fewer than two outs?

If there's a guy on base coming behind you, you want to try and extend the play as long as possible, running back and forth without

186

getting tagged out, so he can end up on second base, in scoring position. That's your job in this situation. So even if you are put out in the rundown, you'll still have a runner in **scoring position** when the next batter comes to the plate.

Once you know he has made it safely to second, after that, you just do your best to get to third. But your chances are pretty slim.

    GLOSSARY

GLOSSARY

Banana curve: A path the runner takes along the first-base line on a base hit. The baserunner runs straight for a while, then bends to the right into foul territory before circling back to touch the inside of the first-base bag. This creates a straighter angle to go to second base on the play.

Bang-bang play: A close safe-or-out play on the bases.

Beating it out: Making it safely to the base.

Gap: The space between the outfielders, called left-center and right-center, respectively.

Good read: A good understanding.

Jump: A quick start toward a target.

Picking up: Looking for and finding a particular target.

Running through the bag: Continuing to run hard until you have passed first base.

Scoring position: A runner on either second or third base is considered to be in scoring position because it is possible for the runner to score from either base on any kind of hit.

Two for the Price of One!

Carlton Fisk was a very good catcher for the Boston Red Sox and the Chicago White Sox. He was so good in his twenty-four years in the big leagues that he was inducted into the Hall of Fame in Cooperstown, New York, in 2000. But in all of the games he caught in his long career, one of his most bizarre plays came on August 2, 1985, at Yankee Stadium.

It all began harmlessly enough in the bottom of the seventh, with the score tied at 3–3. Bobby Meacham was on second and Dale Berra was on first, for the Yankees. Rickey Henderson hit a long drive to left-center field. The Chicago center fielder, Luis Salazar, gave chase. Meacham held up, thinking the ball would be caught. But not Berra…he was running hard from the start. When the ball fell safely, Meacham finally began to run hard. Berra was right on his tail. Third-base coach Gene Michael waved Meacham home, and gave Berra the "stop sign" to stay put at third. But Berra was motoring around the base too fast to stop.

When the ball was relayed home to the plate, Fisk slapped a tag on Meacham. And then, reacting quickly, he dove and tagged out Berra, too. Instead of a possible rally, New York did not score. The Yankees ultimately lost the game, 6–5!

★ ★

HERE'S THE SITUATION

Your team is trailing by four runs and it's the last inning. You're leading off, and you hit a ball into the gap in right-center. The ball falls safely for a hit. As you round first base, you think you might have a chance to make it to second.

Should you try for a double?

HERE'S THE SOLUTION

It's always good to be aggressive on the basepaths. But you also have to be smart.

If you are going to try for a double, you should be 100 percent certain that you can make it safely. At that point in the game, your run doesn't mean as much compared to the risk you're taking by trying for the extra base. You always want to get into scoring position. But the gamble to make it safely to second is probably not worth it because your team is down four runs. Take the single and hope your hit starts a big rally.

Now, if you were one run down in the same situation, you might want to take a chance and try for the double. If you make it safely, your team will have the tying run in scoring position with no one out

★★ Carl Crawford's Memories ★★

I PLAYED in the Eastmont Houston [Texas] Little League. Those were fun days. We won state championships all the time. I played for the Angels. That was the name of our team.

I was a first baseman and a pitcher. Back then I was a good pitcher. I just threw the ball right down the middle. That was it. It was good playing first base. In Little League it's boring not to play in the infield, so I was just happy to not be in the outfield. I was left-handed so I couldn't play any of the other positions, and I wanted to be in the mix, so first base was the only thing I could do.

I batted third or fourth. I was hitting for power back then. I used to hit home runs all the time in Little League.

After a tournament game or something like that we might go somewhere to eat and do something, but for the most part after we played we just went home and relaxed.

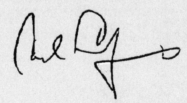

THE FINAL PITCH

By now you're probably ready to race back out to the diamond, fueled by all the information you've learned from this book. But remember, you won't become a Derek Jeter or a CC Sabathia overnight! They weren't the big league stars they are now when they were your age, either.

Whether you're hitting the field for practice or playing a game, keep in mind the tips these twenty pros have offered. Their advice will help you to improve your skills and become the best baseball player you can be. And as you pick up your glove and bat and head out to the field, remember one other very important thing. Baseball is just a game. Yes, you always want to play hard in a game. And you play to help your team win. But here's the tip on which every big league player seems to agree, whether he's a pitcher, catcher, infielder, outfielder, or hitter: enjoy the game!

That's something the late Hall of Famer Willie Stargell did throughout his superb career with the Pittsburgh Pirates. "Pops," as he was called, never forgot the first baseball lesson he ever learned. "Baseball's supposed to be fun," Stargell often said. "The [umpire] says 'Play ball,' not 'Work ball,' you know." So get out to the field and have fun!

ABOUT THE AUTHOR

STEVEN KRASNER was a sports writer for the *Providence Journal* for thirty-three years, covering the Boston Red Sox on a daily basis from 1986 until his retirement in 2008. He is a graduate of Columbia University, where he played baseball and was team captain and MVP in his senior year. Krasner is the author of PLAY BALL LIKE THE PROS: TIPS FOR KIDS FROM 20 BIG LEAGUE STARS; PLAY BALL LIKE THE HALL OF FAMERS: THE INSIDE SCOOP FROM 19 BASEBALL GREATS; PEDRO MARTINEZ; WHY NOT CALL IT COW JUICE?; THE LONGEST GAME; and HAVE A NICE NAP, HUMPHREY. He conducts interactive and motivational writing workshops called "Nudging the Imagination" (www.nudgingtheimagination.com) in schools and at conferences across the country and is a member of the Baseball Hall of Fame's Education Advisory Council. He lives in Rhode Island.

ACKNOWLEDGMENTS

Tyler Beckstrom; Nick Cafardo; Greg Casterioto, Philadelphia Phillies; Peter Chase, Chicago Cubs; Chris Costello, Tampa Bay Rays; Jerry Crasnick; Brooke Dobbins; George Patrick Duffy; Pam Ganley, Boston Red Sox; Ariele Goldman, New York Yankees; Kevin Gregg, Philadelphia Phillies; Charlie Hepp, Colorado Rockies; Mike Herman, Minnesota Twins; Danielle Holmes, Chicago Cubs; Michael Ivins, Boston Red Sox; Mike Kennedy, Minnesota Twins; Tim Kurkjian; Michael Maas; Carmen Molina, Tampa Bay Rays; Alan Nero; Brian Peters; Mark Rogoff, Los Angeles Dodgers; Ken Rosenthal; Erik Ruiz, Tampa Bay Rays; Jim Salisbury, Jayson Stark; Tateki "Bori" Uchibori, Tampa Bay Rays; Rick Vaughn, Tampa Bay Rays; Bobby Witt, Jason Zillo, New York Yankees.

Bill Almon; Bill Arnold; John Blake, Texas Rangers; Fred Bowen; Dick Bresciani, Boston Red Sox; Rob Butcher, Cincinnati Reds; Megan Dimond, Philadelphia Phillies; Bill Gates, National Baseball Hall of Fame & Museum; Monique Giroux, Montreal Expos; Sean Harlin, Minnesota Twins; Diane Hock; Peggy Jackson; Emily Krasner; Tim Mead, Anaheim Angels; Gerard and Jeff Ratigan; Scott Reifort, Chicago White Sox; Matt Roebuck, Seattle Mariners; Kevin Shea, Boston Red Sox; Jay Stenhouse, Toronto Blue Jays; Bill Stetka, Baltimore Orioles; Bart Swain, Cleveland Indians; Leigh Tobin, Philadelphia Phillies; David Witty, Kansas City Royals.

Peachtree Publishers: Jessica Alexander, Kate DePalma, Marian Gordin, Loraine Joyner, Vicky Holifield, Kathy Landwehr, Melanie McMahon Ives, and Maureen Withee.